BE STILL

BE STILL

LARRY B. REESE

For additional copies, visit www.lulu.com.

Cover and Interior Design by Greer Wymond | www.thecreativebird.com

Edited by a very good brother who gifted me with his skills and wishes to remain anonymous. To him I am very thankful!

ISBN: 978-1-312-27109-8

Scripture quotations are taken from:
The Amplified Bible, Expanded Edition
Copyright © 1987 by the Zondervan Corporation and the Lockman Foundation.

For all the students who have gone through the Discipleship School, are in the school presently, and to those who will go through the school.

BE STILL

FOREWORD

Twenty-first century Christians live under cultural, techno-
logical and social conditions that are vastly removed from
those of our forbears in the fledging Church. Yet in so many
important respects we are no different from them at all. While
scrolls may have been replaced by tablet computers and smart
phones, and while we now get around in minivans and SUVs instead of by donkey or camel, in our nature we are the just same
as the earliest believers. Where the heart of man is concerned,
there is truly nothing new under the sun.

The same things that were indispensable to nurture the spirits of Paul and Silas and Mary and Martha are just as needful for
us two thousand years later in the digital age. One of the most
essential disciplines for all followers of Christ, whether facing
persecution from the Roman Empire or a more modern "tyranny
of the urgent," is to learn to be still, to quiet our hearts and minds
before God, and to listen carefully for His voice in the midst of
whatever circumstances may impose themselves on us. Brother

Larry Reese brings that much needed but often neglected practice into sharp focus in *Be Still.*

As a recent student of Brother Larry, and as one who has
benefited greatly from his teaching of the Word and heart of God
both in his discipleship school and in his earlier books, it is with
great enthusiasm that I commend this newest title to your reading. *Be Still* is abundant in practical scriptural truth, expounded
by an author whose heart overflows with love for God and His
people. Larry is at once a spiritual mentor and a beloved brother
in the Lord, whose gentle demeanor often gives way to his
unquenchable passion to help his fellow believers know Jesus
in an intimate and transformational way. This book will help you
make great strides to that end. May the God of all grace be with
you as you read.

David E. Johnson
Rivers Crossing Discipleship School Alumnus

1

BE STILL

Noise. Wherever I go there seems to be so much noise. Hurry. So many people seem to be in a hurry and really do not know why they're in a hurry. It seems that with the advancement of technology, we've grown more and more impatient, less tolerant of others, and don't seem to get as much done as we use to. Well, we do get a lot done, but it seems as if it still takes a lot of time away from what is important. Many families seem to spend less and less time together and more and more time either in front of the television or some screen, chatting with or texting someone who could sometimes greatly benefit from a phone call—a personal call, where the other person can hear our voice and its varying fluctuations so that the communication is more personal. Sadly, our rushing world and all the things that take so much of our time interfere with our relationship with our heavenly Father also. Nothing is wrong with technology as long as it does not interfere with our much needed intimacy with God. We need to be quiet sometimes and to sit alone with Father to see what He has to speak to us. Knowing that God speaks to us in such a way, gives us the assurance that we can count on Him to assist us in our busyness throughout the day and that we can depend on Him to help us get things done without all the hassle that often comes in our "rat race" world. The ability to be quiet and to sit still with our heavenly Father does amazing things within us. So many of us are working so hard to get things done that we fail to really know that our Father in heaven is interested in our progress and wants to help us. But we need to be still and to learn the importance of why we need to be still and what happens when we are still before God.

Our lives are filled with situations that seem to demand an answer or insist on an outcome that we are not always prepared to handle, and even our technology is limited in taking care of the situations in our lives that tend to weigh on the emotional aspects of our lives. There is no button that we can press or any I-pad instrument that can assist us when our needs become emotional.

Sadly, the use of so much technology has made many of us robotic in our approach to people, often lacking intimacy in relationships, causing even those who are closest to us to sometimes feel alone or lonely. What can be done about this busyness that seems to take almost every waking hour of our day? There must be something that we can do to settle inwardly and to recognize that, as Christians, there is a better way to quiet the storm or storms in our lives that seem to go on and on. Often, we lack belief and faith that God has designed for us to have peace even in a busy world. Sometimes we need only be still.

God is the One Who gives us work to do. He is the One Who requires us to work, but He does not want us to work ourselves to death. From my own personal experience with God, I have learned that He wants to work along with us, affirming us in our work, so that we can sense the faithful assurance from God that He is indeed with us. We must not forget that God wants us to receive pleasure in what we do, and along with this pleasure, our Father wants us to know from Him that He is pleased with what we do, that is, if we are doing what Father created and designed us to do.

*"...For we are fellow workman (joint promoters, laborers together) with and for God..." **1 CORINTHIANS 3:9***

So it is good to know, recognize, and to bear in mind that we are working along with God, creating and doing great things that only we are designed to do. God determined we should do well ahead of our knowing it. The key to having success with and enjoying work or intimate fellowship with God is to be able to know 'where' to find Him and how to 'find' that place of rest in Him when everything around us seems to be going haywire. The person who has trained himself to sit still before God is able to tune out all the noise that is around him, able to focus directly on God, no matter what is happening around him or how difficult things may be emotionally. Once we learn to go straight to God and to live in His presence, so much good comes from our being quiet within. A person who sits with God and learns to recognize His voice is a better minister to others, because he isn't simply speaking what he believes will help another, but what God is actually putting in his heart at the moment. Being still before God empowers us to know what Father is speaking to us by His Holy Spirit at the moment, giving us insight that the person in front of us needs at that very moment. This cannot be done when we find ourselves hurried and pushed along with the day's activities and whatever demands our time, —so what can we do to quiet this unending rush?

> *"...Let be and be still, and know (recognize and understand) that I am God..." **PSALM 46:10***

It is possible to turn away from the things that constantly bombard us, often making it seem that everything else is urgent and requires our immediate attention; however, when we become still before the Lord, desiring His input and refusing to move forward without it, we find that our Father has a very strong and definitive presence, and wants to involve Himself; however, He wants to be invited to help. He wants to feel welcomed into our lives to help us.

Being still takes time. It is not until we are actually sitting still that we realize how nervous and jittery the day has made us, and often, this is at the very end of the day. It is usually at the very end of the day when we have nothing left, and wanting to spend time with God is the last thing on our minds, and if it is, it doesn't come with a strong enough desire to actually spend considerable time with Him. I'm not speaking of the volume of time that we spend with Father, but the quality of time we spend with Him. Oftentimes we find that spending time with our heavenly Father gives us mental and spiritual energy that we did not have before we actually sat down to spend time with Him. Yes, I know that our bodies and minds get tired, but Father has a way of restoring or giving energy back into our tired souls. The true challenge will be to come to a place during the day where we are certainly still before the Lord while realizing that we do not have to be in a special place to hear God. It is not necessarily the position of our body when we are still before God, but it is the receptivity of our hearts. Can we hear Father no matter what is going on around us? Yes, if we learn to be properly still before Him.

~~2

LET BE

W e have already seen in Chapter 1 that the Psalmist wrote:

> *"Let be and be still, and know (recognize and understand) that I am God."* **PSALM 46:10**

If we are ever going to be able to recognize that God is Who He says He is in the avenues of our lives, we have to learn to cultivate the ability to let things alone; to be still after letting those things alone; and to wait on Father's voice to give us instruction or to simply give us peace. Whatever God chooses to do will always be fine with us the more we learn that He is for us and not against us. Bear in mind as we move forward that God is co-laboring with us. He is not fighting against us; however, if we are going in the wrong direction, He will put up road blocks to keep us from being harmed. It is wise to be sensitive to the possibility of these roadblocks.

What does it mean to let something be? Simply put, it means to come to a place where we are not trying to cause or make something happen with whatever is bothering us or controlling certain areas of our lives. Many times in ministry I find people who are actively engaged in trying to change situations or people who cause them problems. This can become very tiring, depressing, and discouraging, often leading us to pray and pray about something that God doesn't seem to be doing anything about. There are times when our heavenly Father will move rather quickly on the things that are bothering us and other times, He may choose to leave them as they are. We learn our greatest lessons in waiting on our heavenly Father to move on our requests. During these waiting times, it would be wise to simply let be, to not be distracted by what seems to be so urgent and demanding, and simply trust God.

We see in the first chapter of Habakkuk how he was complaining to God about how the leaders in Judah are oppressing the poor, and so he asks God why He allows the wicked to prosper. It is important to understand that it is alright to complain to God—in fact, it is healthy to learn how to complain to God, rather than complain against Him. When we complain to God it gives Him an open door by which He can answer us, to make His position known, and to even correct us if our thinking is wrong. Here in the second chapter we see what Habakkuk did once he had made his complaint known to God.

"...Oh, I know, I have been rash to talk out plainly this way to God! I will [in my thinking] stand upon my post of observation and station myself on the tower or fortress, and will watch to see

what He will say within me and what answer I will make [as His
mouthpiece] to the perplexities of my complaint against Him."
HABAKKUK 2:1

Habakkuk, once he had complained to God, he then became
silent and waited for God to answer him. First we must believe
that once we have complained to Father that we allow some
quiet time (or being still) time before Him so that He may answer
us. While we can tell that Habakkuk is emotionally attached to
his complaint to God, we must also understand that sometimes
when we are too emotionally attached to something, it can keep
us from receiving a clear answer from God. In other words, we
could very easily get a mixed answer. What we hear could be
partially us because we are too close to the situation. For this
reason, it is necessary that we distance ourselves as much as
possible from a situation until we feel quiet enough on the inside
to hear God speak to us about it. After we have practiced this
long enough, we will find that hearing Father speak even in difficult situations becomes easier.

The next thing we must do after we have quieted ourselves
in the presence of God is to expect Him to answer. When He
answers, we should be willing to do what He instructs us to do,
should there be any instruction. The proper way to listen to God
is to hear what He is saying with the intention of obeying, and not
looking for a second opinion. Father's answer will include instructions for us to follow that we either may not like or have to wait
to see what He actually does. Either way, being still is required to
hear what He has to say to us. Once Father gives us instructions
we can be sure that He will give us the ability to carry out what

He wants us to do. This principle of hearing God while we are still before Him works in any given situation. We may not always find ourselves assailed with troubles and problems that require we hear right away from God. Sometimes nothing is wrong at all and being able to hear Father speak strengthens us in our hearts, simply for the point of encouragement for ourselves or for someone else who may need it.

> "...Be still and rest in the Lord; wait for Him and patiently lean yourself upon Him..." **PSALM 37:7**

Rest comes from simply being with God because God does address the things that trouble us. The Scriptures teach us that if we acknowledge God in all the things we do, He will direct and lead us in the right pathway but this knowledge of how He does it comes with time and a understanding of Who God is and who we are as His children. God's way of doing things can be mysterious to us as we are growing to know Him, but as we maintain steadfastness and patience, we begin to see that God is Who He says He is and rewards those who are diligent in their pursuit of obedience to Him.

The more we develop the desire to obey Father, the more we will find the rest that is spoken of in Psalm 37. Rest comes supernaturally as we yield our hearts to God, desiring to be with Him and to hear what He has to say on a matter just as Habakkuk did. It is important to God that we know how to communicate whatever we feel, having this understanding that just because we may believe something doesn't mean it is true, and if what we believe is negatively affecting the way that we feel, then our feelings must change as we begin to think the right way. We cannot lack wisdom if we are seeking to be with God alone—just for Him. As we grow to know God for God, we also develop in wisdom, insight, and understanding of God, which enables us to be still before Him. As we practice implementing the desire to be still when we are with God, the more we will recognize where our Father is.

3 ⎯⎮⎮⎯

FINDING REST

"...Return to your rest, O my soul, for the Lord has dealt bountifully with you." **PSALM 116:7**

If we are going to find rest in our busy lives, then we must really know that rest is possible, and that rest comes from being still with our heavenly Father. I know that our Father's very breath is resuscitative, if we sit with Him long enough, we realize that His words give life. Jesus spoke the words that lead to eternal life, or the life that comes with walking in the new nature or spiritual life that we now have as those who believe God. Believing God is essential to enjoying this new life that He speaks of, but belief alone doesn't get us into the place of rest with God—we must exercise faith in what we believe. For instance, if we say that we believe God is able to do a certain thing and when the opportunity comes in life to really trust Him to do what He says, we must rely on our faith in what God has said to see Him act upon His word. Oftentimes, we want to see our heavenly Father perform miracles, when the truth is if we live by faith each day in God and in His word, then we simply feel closer to the occurrence and possibility of miracles because we are actually sensitive to God's presence. Reading the Bible all the time and quoting certain passages of Scripture often do not necessarily make us closer to God—it is what we believe about God in our hearts, and acting upon what we believe where faith in God is generated from the mind into our experience with God.

Rest is important because resting with God quiets our hearts. This kind of rest allows us to really feel that God is near, and it prepares us to hear what Father is going to say to us, much like with Habakkuk. We can see that Habakkuk made his complaint to God and was intelligent enough and had faith enough in God to know that He would answer Him. We must have this same expectation if we are going to hear clearly from God. Be still with God. Be silent with Him. Expect Him to do something, not in our timing, but in His.

We are told in Psalm 23:

"The Lord is my Shepherd [to feed, guide, and shield me], I shall not lack. He makes me lie down in [fresh, tender] green pastures; He leads me beside the still and restful waters. He refreshes and restores my life (myself); He leads me in the paths of righteousness [uprightness and right standing with Him—not for my earning it, but] for His name's sake." **VERSES 1–3**

As a shepherd, David understood the importance of sheep feeling safe and kept from harm. He also understood that sheep depended upon the shepherd for safety. Because David understood this, he also understood the need to put his full trust in God—relying on Him whenever he felt nervous, harassed, unsure, unsafe, and then relying on God to help him. It is very important dear ones that we begin to find our place as Father's children as soon as possible, and that can only be done when we are spending careful and definitive time with Him. We learn to find rest from all the distractions and demands of this life when we come before the Lord with our whole hearts. This is a process that can be very difficult in the beginning of our becoming more acquainted with God. All of us have the tendency to develop our relationships with each other based upon trust. We do not go into relationships trusting the other person wholeheartedly; this would be foolish and could be very detrimental to us, but even so, the risk factor of being hurt by someone remains. There is no one person that we can trust completely as far as never disappointing us and letting us down. We can only find this kind of security in Christ our Savior, so if we are to have a vision for life in this world from God, we must develop our relationship with our Lord Jesus Christ.

In the beginning lines of Psalm 23, David says that the Lord is his Shepherd and that He will feed, guide, and shield him. Because he has placed his confidence in God, he knows that God will care for him. But again we must realize that David had to get to know God before he realized from experience with God that He would do the things he wrote about in this psalm. David further says that God will refresh and restore his life. If we are going to live in society and do well, we must understand that there will be many challenges that come at us in varying ways; however, if we know how to find rest in being with God, then living in this world will be easier. Our focus must be on our heavenly Father and what He desires. We must understand that in this focus on God, we must completely rely on what Father wants from us, and not what we can offer Him.

The most reasonable thing that we can give to our heavenly Father is ourselves. We are to give God ourselves because it was the giving away of ourselves to follow after Satan that led us out of rest with our heavenly Father in the beginning. That is why the psalmist says in our open passage: 'Return to your rest, O my soul, for the Lord has dealt bountifully with you.' For the Lord to deal bountifully with us, we must be willing to come to Him, just as the sheep come to their beloved shepherd, the one they are sure will help them. They rely on the shepherd, and when they cry out, they are crying out to him in a tone that lets him know that something isn't quite right. If we are going to cry out to our heavenly Father in a 'tone' that lets Him know that something isn't quite right, then we must realize and recognize that He is indeed our Shepherd, and He hears us when things are not right.

We must also know that God may not always run to our immediate aid. This usually occurs more and more as we grow older in our relationship with Him. This is true because even as an infant grows older, the mother recognizes the urgency of his or her cry. She can tell when something is really wrong with her child because she has grown to recognize certain pitches and the language behind the cry of her child. So is it with God. Our Father will speak certain truths to us as we listen to Him, and if we are really listening to Him and absorbing what He is saying in our hearts, then we will have peace and rest and quiet. These times of peace, rest, and quiet are intended to form and shape our hearts for what will eventually come into our lives. There is no life without some kind of trouble. Hurt and disappointment will eventually come into our lives, and the important thing is that we are ready for those things as the Father prepares us for them.

If we are to say that we are to return to rest, then we must understand that there are some things that make us restless in life, so we must begin to find that place with God where He is able to quiet and calm us, to restore and make us whole again after something has shaken us. I want us to remember that Satan will come to steal, to kill, and to destroy whatever the Father brings into our lives for our good. His damaging desire is to keep us frightened, upset, and to feel as if we are orphans, rather than true children of God. Satan will, if he can, torment us constantly with fears that we cannot shake on our own, and it is for this reason that we spend time with Father, growing not only to know His voice, but His presence in the times of trouble that all of us will eventually encounter. But don't be afraid of the promise that Satan will come to try and steal what Father has put within us. We must remember that Satan is threatened by the maturing Christian, the one who is growing to know God better, and the way that this begins to happen is by a coming away from all that distracts in this world into a quiet place that Father has already prepared within Himself, so that we may find help when we need it.

"...Looking away [from all that will distract] to Jesus, Who is the Leader and the Source of our faith [giving the first incentive for our belief] and is also it's Finisher [bringing it to maturity and perfection]." HEBREWS 12:2A

In the walk with our heavenly Father, remember and know that we are His children, and we have full access to Him through Jesus Christ. Nothing must shake us from knowing this. As we maintain this growing knowledge in our hearts, the fears and distractions that Satan often bombards us with will lose their power over us, but we must keep our eyes on Jesus, especially when things come into our lives that seem unfair. It is during the times when things happen to us that seem unfair that we begin to question, and often we will question God for allowing such things to happen and why He did; however, the question is not necessarily why God allowed it to happen, but the fact that it has happened, and what do we do about it for God's greater glory.

Dear ones, there are things that will happen to all of us in life, no matter how good we think we've been. If we are going to be victorious and continue to live in peace and rest with God, we have to know that certain things serve an eternal purpose, and it is up to us, leaning on Father's arms and listening to Him for wisdom that we know the difference. Not everything that happens to us is pleasant, but we can know how these difficult things can make us more powerful in our walk with God in life now, here on earth, where such things are going to happen.

> *"The thief comes only in order to steal and kill and destroy. I came that they may have and enjoy life, and have it in abundance (to the full, till it overflows)." JOHN 10:10*

As a believer in Jesus Christ, we will have to come to the place where we really believe that Satan is out to destroy us, and in any way that he can. He does not play fair. He does not care about any person, including infants, little children, the elderly, the sick. He cares for no one. In truth, he is the epitome of evil, everything that is not God, Satan epitomizes. It can be easy to simply believe this without ever having an experience in life that reveals Satan as our truest enemy. He will do whatever he can to harm us at whatever cost, that is, if our heavenly Father allows it. We must understand here that wherever there is an opportunity for Satan to harm us, he will do it, and he looks for such opportunities.

I remember some years ago when my mother had several heart attacks back to back. It was the most traumatic time of my life. It was probably the most vulnerable time in my life as a Christian, when I felt so helpless to do anything to help my mother, watching for a few moments as the doctors struggled to save her life, then they suddenly shouted: "Get him out of here!" My mother lay there on the emergency room bed at the mercy of the expertise of the doctors attending her. This isn't a sight that I'd want anyone to have, but it happens. Sadly, this kind of scene is part of the world we live in and it is no respecter of persons.

I remember leaving the hospital, headed home, nervously shaking on the inside, waiting to hear what was going to happen to my dear mother. I loved my mother more than any other human being in this world, and seeing her powerless there for those few moments haunted me. I remember how Satan tormented me in my thoughts and was able to do so because I was so tired, exhausted, so I could barely battle against him. My mind was too occupied with what my mother had gone through, and what I had seen in the emergency room. The thoughts kept coming back over and over in my mind like a mini movie that just wouldn't end, and each time the vision of what I'd seen came into my mind, I felt all the more exhausted and helpless. But I did not feel hopeless. I knew that God was with me during this time, even though I had not been able to hear Him speak to me during this entire episode. But the devil was speaking to me in my weakness.

"Look at what He did to your Mama," he said to me in an aggressive voice that affirmed his viciousness to me and the condition my mother was in. "Look at what He did. She's dead, dead!" I want you to imagine what hearing this did to me during what I maintain was the most horrible day in my life—the day that my mother was put on life preservation equipment, when there was no brain activity. She was simply lying there, only breathing with the help of a machine. Satan, who is an opportunist and strategist against us and our Father, caused rushing thoughts of lost hope through my mind.

We can believe that when our Savior was in the wilderness being tempted by Satan, He went through something very similar, but His help came from knowing Who He was and knowing Who God had called Him to be. His response to Satan assures us of this truth. He would not give up His identity or His purpose so that Satan could have the rule over Him. He maintained what the Scriptures say about God and those who are His children. Remember that in any battle with Satan, the truth of God never changes, no matter what the circumstances look like or dictate.

At this point in my life, I did not know everything that Father had planned for me or the way that He would carry out and reveal His plans to me. I did know that I was a threat to Satan because of my faith in Jesus. Satan was attempting to use my mother's illness to torment me by speaking lies to my mind that God wasn't real or loving, that He had allowed my mother to die on purpose. Satan was able to war this battle in my mind because he knew that I loved my mother next to God, and he was using this love for my mom to make me believe that God didn't care. It did not work.

"Father, help me," I cried out to God. I remember being so tired that I could no longer fight Satan's lies in my mind. He was vicious and determined to make me feel that God was totally responsible for what was happening, but I resolved that it wasn't the truth. Dear ones, if we truly spend quality time with Father, we begin to know His true nature, that He is altogether love. We learn this by the language He uses and what He shares with us about Himself personally. We cannot discover truth about God simply because we look for it—God reveals truth about Himself as we seek Him. There is something about the way that Father reveals truth about Himself. The words that He shares goes straight to our hearts, enlarging our view of Father and giving us insight into Who He really is. It is for this reason that we need to understand that it is not what happens when we talk to God, but what happens when He talks to us. As Father reveals Himself to us we begin to know Him and how to talk to Him, it is also in this place of communication that we learn to know His voice and to rest in what He says.

I know that it was because of the intimate time that I had spent with Father that Satan was not able to get me to take the bait of his lie, that my heavenly Father had caused this terrible thing to happen to my mother. As I called out to God, I could not feel much of a response from Him until I slowed down, stopped running from the thoughts of Satan and trying to force them out of mind, and simply became still—yes, still and quiet. When I stopped running and began to allow my mind to focus on how Father had always been faithful to me, I suddenly knew that there was no difference in His possible response now, even though I'd never experienced anything like this in my life. I slowly lowered myself from the inside, and rested on what I knew was His inner strength. The attack from Satan seemed to lighten, and I said to God, "I'm too tired. I'm too weak. Please make him stop." It was after I spoke these few words to Father that I began to feel His peace come over me in a very dramatic way—unlike I'd never felt it before. But I knew that it was because I had, in this horrible battle with Satan, submitted my heart to Father's. I surrendered myself to the only strength that had been available to me all this time. I believed God. I trusted that He would help, but I had to allow what I believed to fall over on His faithfulness so that I could see it for myself. Within a very short time I became so peaceful, so quiet, that I did not understand this kind of heaviness of peace that flooded my soul. It went past any peace I'd ever felt, and it was appropriate for what was happening. It stopped the attack, and what was once a loud and unrelenting attack of Satan, came to a stand still, and his voice faded in the peace and quiet of my Father's presence.

When we experience this kind of peace with God, we do not want to let it go. While we may not always have this kind of spiritual peaceful experience with God, it may not always be needed to this degree. Father gave me the peace that was necessary for the attack of Satan against me. I was able to find rest in Father, but the key was I had to find the position of Father within myself, going to the place where the Holy Spirit responds to faith and truth. Whenever we are held asunder by the devil's attacks or difficulties in life period, there is a place within that the Father has placed Himself as a resident. As we learn to lean over on Him in any situation that robs us of rest and peace, we find rest in Him. We find that there is no storm or situation that is too difficult for our Father's peace to intervene and cause us rest. I remember the peace of God was strong over me during that time that I fell asleep, resting more deeply than I can ever remember resting and when I awoke, I felt as if it had been a dream of some kind, but knew that only God could have put me to sleep and stopped Satan's attacks so completely.

> "...And God's peace [shall be yours, that tranquil state of a soul assured of its salvation through Christ, and so fearing nothing from God and being content with its earthly lot of whatever sort that is, that peace] which transcends all understanding shall garrison and mount guard over your hearts and minds in Christ Jesus."
> **PHILIPPIANS 4:7**

> "You are a hiding place for me; You Lord, preserve me from trouble, You surround me with songs and shouts of deliverance."
> **PSALM 32:7A**

> "So be subject to God, Resist the devil [stand firm against him], and he will flee from you. Come close to God and He will come close to you..." **JAMES 4:7, 8A**

⌁ 4

DYING TO SELF

henever death is talked about, there always seems to be some kind of fear associated with it. Are we afraid of death itself or simply the process by which we may die? Are we simply afraid of what we do not know or understand about death? Why is there often such mystery associated with death? This truth also applies to dying to ourselves to truly walk in the new nature we now have in Christ. The Scriptures tell us that when we become new creatures in Christ the old things pass away and all things become new. This doesn't mean that we no longer have a past associated with our lives or that the bad things we've done simply disappear, but it means that our old spiritual condition is no longer alive. And for something to die, it must be killed by some means or die on its own; however, for the old spiritual condition to die, it must be subjected to the nature of God. The question is, how does this work? Let's look at two passages of Scripture.

"Therefore if any person is [ingrafted] in Christ (the Messiah) he is a new creation (a new creature altogether); the old [previous moral and spiritual condition] has passed away. Behold, the fresh and new has come!" **2 CORINTHIANS 5:17**

"And you [He made alive], when you were dead (slain) by [your] trespasses and sins in which at one time you walked [habitually]." **EPHESIANS 2:1,2A**

As we mature in our relationship with God, we better understand that we do not become more spiritually strong, assertive, and responsive to God simply because we want to. In earnest, there is no other way to cooperate with God other than by interacting with Him spiritually. Our heavenly Father is Spirit and must be worshiped in spirit and in truth. When we talk about truth, we are talking about the Spirit of our heavenly Father, the Holy Spirit, Who only speaks, gives, and represents truth, and especially the truth about God. For we cannot come to God simply because we decide to come to Him, but we come to our Father and are drawn to Him as the Holy Spirit gives us the ability to do so. Our relationship with God is sustained by our growing knowledge of Who He is as given to us by being intimate with the Holy Spirit. The question here, then, is how do we become intimate with something or someone that we cannot see?

The writer of Corinthians speaks to us about the process by which we become more acquainted with God and how we die to our natural, unrenewed selves.

"[I assure you] by the pride which I have in you in [your fellowship and union with] Christ Jesus our Lord, that I die daily [I face death every day and die to self]." **1 CORINTHIANS 15:31**

You have heard me share that God is spirit and for us to interact with God in spirit, we cannot see Him as He is and continue to live in the same morally depraved spirit. The condition of man without the influence of the Holy Spirit is called "flesh." It is the condition of man without the life transforming power of the Holy Spirit. If we are going to die to ourselves the way that Father intends, we must surrender to the Holy Spirit. Of course, I realize that many of us struggle with what we need to do so that this process moves along quickly; however, our Father does not always allow things to happen quickly. He is not like us. Whatever experiences we have with God are meant to teach us more about ourselves and about Himself. The lessons that our Father wants us to learn are not always learned quickly. That is why our Father prescribes certain tests and trials for each of us that are tailored to our own personal individuality. God knows us far better than we know ourselves. He knows what we are supposed to be in life, so His initial dealing with our salvation is to lead us into understanding destiny and purpose, and part of this has to do with the dying of ourselves.

The Holy Spirit is well aware of the path that our Father has chosen for us to follow. He is and listens to God. He protects and watches over everything that concerns God, and so He is quite able to complete that which Father has invested in us by His Holy Spirit, including teaching us how to die to ourselves. How, then, does He do this?

If we look at the life of our dear Savior, Jesus, then we will better understand how this dying to self process proceeds and leads us to be more like Jesus. When I say to be more like Jesus, I mean in His spiritual demeanor, that is, to always obey the Father and conform to His will. The best way not to sin habitually is to have the Spirit of God operating in us in a mature capacity, where we are no longer subjected to persistent weakness from our flesh, or the nature of man without the influence of the Holy Spirit.

Of course, many of us know that when we sin or do what we consider sinning against God, there is a penalty for that sin. We feel it inside. We feel like we have done something wrong in our minds, and we believe that God will eventually 'get' us for the sin we've committed. The truth of the matter is if we do not come to God the same way as when we first met Him, then we will continue to fear punishment from Him. Why is it important not to run from God or try to justify sin when we do sin? Because the more we come to God when we do sin, the more we realize His love for us and His ability to separate us from the sin we commit, and we better understand the full sacrifice of Jesus Christ for our sin. In honesty, sin is no longer the major problem we have as believers because God has already done something about that in Himself (represented) by Jesus Christ having died on the cross. His primary concern is that we have faith in Him to continue cleansing us from sin from that day forward. The more we confess, the more we have the potential to see God in our lives. We do not see God more or relate to Him more intimately through confession alone, but by seeking to know Him as Moses did, going past the sin problem into seeing His glory. Listen dear ones, the more we see Christ, the more we die to ourselves, and the more we die to ourselves, the more we see all that God desires to fill us with, and that is with the knowledge of Himself. For us to die to ourselves we must have the assurance that something is on the other side of the life that we die to. We cannot see or have that life unless we die daily as Paul mentioned in Corinthians, and being brought alive in the new nature by what Father reveals to us after death to ourselves. A great advantage that Jesus had in His relationship with God was that He obeyed Him, and this obedience came with faithful insight that Father would care for Him and bring Him back to life, even after a horrible death. This is the kind of faith that Father wants to establish in each of us, the knowledge that there is something else for us on the other side of dying to ourselves. And when I speak of dying to ourselves, I do not mean physical death, but the death of living for our own selves, which keeps us in the state of being separated from knowing God and what His plans are for us. We cannot know what Father's plans are for us by avoiding the death of self.

We have heard God referred to as Father, which means "affectionate One;" however, many of us do not know God as being affectionate. He has to teach us this Himself through the tests and trials that He leads us through personally. Dear ones, it is possible to recognize the trials that our Father prescribes and the ones we bring upon ourselves; however, what matters is not whether Father prescribes the trial or we do something to bring ourselves into trials, but how we respond to God in them. This is what determines our success for future trials and how we are able to learn more about being still within when they occur.

5

BE STILL TO HEAR

"I [the Lord] will instruct you and teach you in the way you should go: I will counsel you with My eye upon you." **PSALM 32:8**

"Great peace have they who love Your law; nothing shall offend them or make them stumble." **PSALM 119:165**

If we are honest with ourselves we will have to admit that we seldom have the peace that we want to have in this world. So many things are competing for our attention, and oftentimes those things that seem to demand so much of our time are the things that win out over our spending time with our Father. I am not promoting a regimen when I speak about spending time with God. I realize that most of us have schedules that are very demanding and limit what we can add to them; however, we should not have to feel that we are adding spending time with God to our schedules. We cannot fit Him in. God should not have to make an appointment to speak with us. It should be the other way around. And remember, when I speak about spending time with God, I am not talking about a lengthy time in a room away from people, shades drawn, soft music playing, and candles lit with some special aroma flowing through the room. This creates a very nice atmosphere, but the truth of the matter is that Father wants our hearts to have this kind of aroma in them, where we desire to be with Him, realizing that being with Him isn't something we are obligated to do but that we are privileged to do. We are told in Scripture that if we will acknowledge God in all that we do—meaning, putting Him first at the beginning of our thought processes before we act, then He will direct our paths. God has a strong desire to instruct us, and we know that He is instructing us when we put faith in what He says and wait on Him. We cannot simply obey what we believe is God's word and then put a time frame on our questions by which our God is to answer. Remember that God is in control and He knows what is going to happen all the time. Our limitations in the area of not knowing what is going to happen often get us into trouble when we impatiently try to make something happen. Fear usually grips our hearts when it doesn't seem as if God is going to do something and we try to make something happen. It isn't wise to plan out things and then—at the end—expect God to honor what we've done. The key to being successful in what we do is to honor God—before we do what we are planning. For as many years as I have been teaching on how to hear God, I have found many students who want to plan everything well ahead of what God may have planned, and then expect Him to honor and bless something that could potentially destroy their lives.

In our opening Scripture we see that those who know God's law or His word have great peace. If we apply what this message means, then we understand that if we know God's word, then we know the Person of the word. I cannot reiterate this enough. It is not enough just to have a head full of Scripture verses that complicate our ability to hear God. That is why we must begin to seek Him, to be quiet before Him, and to master the voices that beckon us to do what we want to do. Sometimes the barrage of voices that come into our minds defeat us and cut any time short that we might want to spend with God. We often give up because there is just too much noise going on in our minds to hear God. If we are going to quiet this noise in our minds, then we must believe that God is interested in what we are doing and wants to speak to us and then engage with us as we carry out His plans. Hear me when I say this: If we are going to follow God, we must get over the fear that we are losing something by following Him. The fear that accompanies obedience can be one or two forms of fear—the fear of God, which is the beginning of wisdom, or that fear that is accompanied by the wisdom of God. The fear of God gives us insight and allows us to have wisdom in the direction that we are taking when we walk with God. It will intensify the more we choose to live by faith. Faith is often accompanied by fear because the mind cannot comprehend what faith is doing and feels out of control. However, to the one who has learned to live by faith, which simply means hearing what Father instructs and then doing it, this fear accompanies that person into a greater walk with God. In other words, this kind of faith brings the assurance face to face that God is involved in what we are doing. Unless we do things God's way, we will not see Him actively involved. Obeying and doing things God's way drastically reduces the time we spend praying, or what we might call praying. Many times what we are doing is simply worrying on our knees, afraid that we are doing the wrong thing and that God is not involved with us, and even if He is involved, we don't seem to feel His presence with us. The person who lives by faith and engages with God has assurance within by the Holy Spirit, Who tells him and assures Him that "I am with you in this." This is why the person who loves the word of God in the Person of Jesus Christ, recognizes that God is with Him. For this person stumbling along his way is very rare, but if he does stumble, the Lord is with him and will pick him up and restore his footing.

The other kind of fear is being afraid of God. This kind of fear tells us that God is not with us and that He is not going to help us. This kind of fear usually has a very loud voice and focuses on past experiences where we have perhaps prayed and God didn't do what we wanted Him to do or what we expected Him to do. This kind of fear is debilitating and keeps us paralyzed until we do something. It can be very similar to Russian roulette where we do not know what is going to happen, but hope for the best. This kind of fear does not promote the will of God, but is a tormenting and dreadful fear. It does not work with faith in God, but hinders it.

Remember that faith and love always work together, and if we are truly living by faith, then love is being produced in us because we see God actively engaging with us in life, produc-ing more faith in our hearts and giving us the ability to know that He is with us. This is why living by faith is so important, it produces the 'sight' that so many of us crave and the affirmation that God is with us. If we read the Scriptures we see that God 'affirmed' Jesus as His Son when He obeyed Him in baptism. We are told that God spoke from a cloud, saying, "This is My Son in Whom I am well pleased." So we see that operating and living by faith pleases God and allows us to feel that affirming pleasure. This kind of living by faith also produces a 'hush' within our busy minds. When we see that God is with us, it becomes very easy to know how to approach God from within and to calm and quiet ourselves to listen to what He may tell us.

Not long ago the Lord spoke to me about moving from an apartment into a house. I have never really liked apartment living, even though the apartment where I lived was very nice. I wanted a house to live in that had an upstairs and extra rooms for guests, should I have them stay the night. When I prayed about the kind of house I wanted, I felt the peace of God in it; in fact, I felt that what I prayed was exactly what Father had put in my heart to pray. I want to say here that whenever God speaks to us, it is His word, and if we are familiar with the written Scriptures, we recognize that it is Father speaking to us. Many times we want Father to "quote" certain Scripture passages to us. This is alright if we know that it is God and have learned to hear Him (speak) the Scriptures. There is a difference between speaking and quoting. God is the Author of His word so He speaks it. To quote something means to borrow it from someone else, and Father doesn't have to do this. This is another reason why it is so important to be still to hear Father. The more we sit still with Him, the more we will recognize the way His presence feels. Feelings are very important to us, but if we are to feel, we want to be sure that our feelings are affected by the truth that our Father speaks to us.

Once I knew what I wanted in a house and what I believed the Lord was putting in me to desire, I entered the information into the search engine on my computer for the area in which I live. Several places came up which promoted some excitement in my heart, so I began to drive around to look at the places I'd found on the computer search—but none of them seemed to fit what I really wanted. Because of the sensitivity that I have to the Holy Spirit, I knew that each house was not the right one even before I drove to it, so I began to feel a bit frustrated. Even though the frustration level wasn't very high, frustration at any level is, well, frustrating. So I went back home and sat still before the Lord. I want to write here that just because our bodies may be still outwardly, it doesn't mean that we are still inwardly. We can be still on the outside but still be emotionally moving inside. This means that we are still very much attached to what we want to see or get done, and this kind of emotional involvement can hinder what Father will tell us. The first important thing in searching for wisdom from God and to being able to be led by Him is to really believe that He wants to help us. We must not allow our minds to continue giving us back up plans, just in case God doesn't speak. Again, this kind of hearing takes time to cultivate.

Second, believe that God is going to reward our search for Him. We must believe that He is God and that He has personal interest in what we are doing or going to do. Acknowledge Him and be willing to hear from Him that what we are doing is not necessarily His will. It is okay to be disappointed when we hear this from God, but the important thing is not to allow this to be terminal, that God does not have a plan when indeed He does. Remember, the pause that we often get from God when He tells us difficult news should not be the end of the conversation. Instead, our Father is giving us the opportunity to compose ourselves emotionally, so that we may continue listening to Him past the point of disappointment. Once we are emotionally composed, then we should continue listening for what the Lord may say next.

"Be still," He said to me. "Keep listening, don't give up." And as I listened to His words, faith was rising in my heart, which enabled me to wait a bit longer to see what He would say. "Go back on-line," He said to me and then told me what city to search in to find the house He wanted me to have and the one that I wanted personally. At first I thought that this particular city was so large and it could very easily put me way out in the country, and I just didn't want to live far out, but my thoughts were based upon what I knew, and not what Father was trying to tell me. So I put a stop to thinking contrary to what Father said and reentered my information into the computer and pressed the city that Father spoke to me about. Immediately homes came up and I saw one in particular that really caught my eye, and I could not get it out of my mind. When I entered the address of the house into map quest to see how far it was from my work, I was pleasantly surprised that it was only four miles. This was a blessing, for sure. But it wasn't until I actually visited the house and walked just inside the front door that I knew it was where Father wanted me to be. Peace and the power of God will always affirm within us that 'this' is the thing that Father wants us to have, but this can only come as we grow to quiet ourselves before God and recognize the way that He does things. Father delights in leading us, but we cannot know this unless we are actively engaged in spending time with Him so that He may reveal Himself to us and to show us what He is like.

> *"The steps of a [good] man are directed and established by the Lord when He delights in his way [and He busies Himself with his every step]. Though he falls, he shall not be utterly cast down, for the Lord grasps his hand in support and upholds him."*
> **PSALM 37:23–24**

6 ⎯⩗⎯

THINGS WE WANT FROM GOD

I think that it is wise to understand how technology often drives us. Sure, it is great to experience the advantage of fast Internet, information at a mouse-click or press of a button, but none of this fast equipment causes our heavenly Father to speed up in the way that He does things. It is often our impatience that makes us in a rush, and a person who is in a rush, is seldom quiet on the inside. Because of our dependency on the fast pace of technology, we often find ourselves in a hurry when we do not need to be. We wake up in the morning, still charged from the night before, and our quick pace doesn't slow down until the week's end. Even then, we are often tired and not able to enjoy the time that we have away from our work. Normally we feel pushed and pressed in life because we believe that running, rushing and hurrying is the only way we can get what we want out of life. Of course, as Christians, we have to believe that the devil is playing the same old trick on us that he played on Adam and Eve in the beginning, and we can see the danger and downfall that it caused them. So it would be wise to conclude that if we practice the same things they practiced before they fell, then the same thing will happen to us if we follow their example. When I say follow their example, I mean to 'miss' the mark or to sin against God as our Father. From what we know in Scripture, the Lord only gave Adam and Eve one thing not to do:

> *"And the Lord God commanded the man, saying, You may freely eat of every tree of the garden; But of the tree of the knowledge of good and evil and blessing and calamity you shall not eat, for in the day that you eat of it you shall surely die."* **GENESIS 2:16–17**

They were not to eat from this particular tree; however, our enemy the devil seduced and caused them to believe that God was actually keeping something from them. Because Adam and Eve were created to have a curiosity from God, they fell prey to the devil's lie and ate from the tree. And ever since that time there has been an innate suspicion within all of us that God is keeping something from us, and that suspicion comes from Satan. One of the reasons why we are often so driven and unable to be still in God's presence is because the desires we have to succeed never seem to go away entirely. We are often engaged, even while resting, with how will we succeed, or how will we get a certain thing done. Now, for a moment I want us to think about what would have happened if Adam and Eve had never believed Satan and eaten from the tree of the knowledge of good and evil. What would have happened if they had simply continued listening to God each day and growing more and more in intimacy with Him? With this kind of relationship with God, Adam and Eve would have grown to know God more as their Father and that He always told them the truth. Then it would have been very difficult for Satan to have deceived them so easily. We know that Satan attacks us early in our walk as Believers in Jesus. He does this because he wants to derail us as soon as possible, causing us to have conflicting views about God and whether He will take care of us or not.

We know that God requires us to work, but He does not want the work that we do to kill us. So many of us are driven to emotional exhaustion because we are constantly trying to 'find' out what we are here for, and to be successful at it. I believe we need to understand that success is really knowing what God wants us to do—what He has put us here for, and doing it to the best of our ability. Oftentimes, we will work ourselves to the place of exhaustion because we don't know whether God (or someone else of influence) in our lives is pleased with our performance. But if we really obey and honor God in our work, doing everything as unto Him, then the Holy Spirit lets us know (now) that we are doing what pleases God and we are able to rest as we do the work. This resting that I am speaking of is not an opportunity for laziness, but it is the understanding that we can have emotional rest when we know what God wants us to do. It is a fringe benefit of knowing that we are in Father's will. So the key to being able to get what we want in life is knowing what God wants us to be in life. Certain work is given to each of us from God, and this work is not designed to simply keep us busy or engaged in activity, but to allow us to feel deeply loved and affirmed by God in what we do. We begin to experience the life that Jesus mentioned we could have, and that is abundant living. Abundant living occurs when we realize that we are not alone in this world, and that our Father is with us from within, giving us instructions as to how we are to live, if we will listen to Him and obey His instructions.

One of the reasons that it is so important to learn how to be still when it comes to getting the things we believe we either need or want from God, is to understand that God wants us to be happy and to be satisfied. It is not the abundance of things that we have that makes us happy; it is how we go about getting those things with Father's help. He intends to show us what we are to do with those things, not so much for His benefit but for the benefit of ourselves and the personal well being of others. If we want to be satisfied in life, then we need to know what God put us here for, and to go about the right way of finding this out from Him. Of course I realize that the culture we live in has programmed us to do and get things a certain way, but our Father is concerned with our knowing how to communicate with Him and to get the best out of that communication. It doesn't simply promote our spirituality and stop there, but knowing God intimately affects every area of our lives, enabling us to enjoy and have fun with Him as our Father and find freedom from being internally rushed as the world teaches us we should be.

It is vitally important that we realize that God wants us to succeed. He doesn't want success to be short-lived, but He wants us to have success as an on going part of being His children. And at the same time, He wants to teach and show us what that success is; that it is not failure when we do not accomplish what we believe we should. If we are going to know how to be still before God, we must recognize that sometimes not winning is a way to learn more about ourselves and to improve in the areas where we are not strong. Knowing this from our Father's point of view will always help us to help others who have the same or similar problems or weaknesses as we do. There is always something to learn and grow from, if our focus is not on succeeding or winning alone.

"He stores up success for honest people." **PROVERBS 27A, NEW INTERNATIONAL READERS VERSION**

It is very important to remember that being still with God is not a waste of time, but saves time. Things give us short-lived returns, but God alone gives us eternal rewards. Investing our faith in God will always bring satisfactory results. As we become acquainted with this truth, we are no longer driven by what is on the outside, which often exhausts us, but we are motivated and led inwardly by the Spirit of our God.

"You open Your hand and satisfy every living thing with favor." **PSALM 145:16**

~~⌐~~ 7

BE STILL MY FEELINGS

"Return to your rest, O my soul, for the Lord has dealt bountifully with you." **PSALM 116:7**

"He leads me beside the still and restful waters." **PSALM 23:2B**

"Do not be conformed to this world (this age), [fashioned after and adapted to its external, superficial customs], but be transformed (changed) by the [entire] renewal of your mind [by its new ideals and its new attitude], so that you may prove [for yourselves] what is the good and acceptable and perfect will of God, even the thing which is good and acceptable and perfect [in His sight for you]." **ROMANS 12:2**

Anyone who studies the Scriptures correctly will see very clearly that the Scriptures always point us to the God of the Scriptures—to the Word of God made flesh, Who came and was sent from God to dwell among us. If our study of the

Scriptures is to be advantageous, then we need to clearly see Jesus reflected in them. If we study the Scriptures for knowledge alone or to try to prove certain arguments, then we will miss the Person of the Scriptures. This is important in our walk with our heavenly Father, if we are going to be able to relate to Him as a Person, as our God. We must come to the place that we know without a doubt and without question that Jesus is the Son of God Who came and walked on the earth—He talked to men, He spent time with men, and revealed what God is like to men. One of the good things to notice in all of this is that Jesus was known well ahead of His time of appearing on the scene as the Christ child, or as the baby Jesus. He appeared to our father Abraham many years before he ever came in the flesh to dwell or live among men for a short 33 years. But the point that I want to make here is that it is easier to communicate with God when we are able to see Jesus as a person, and not limit Him to our memory of Scripture and then reflect that solely upon people. It is easier to represent Jesus our Savior when we know Him—truly, know Him. This means that our study of Scripture, along with careful and intentional prayer should cause us to see our Savior more and more clearly. This cannot be done without the accompanying power of the Holy Spirit. In our experience with the Holy Spirit and studying the Scriptures as we know them, we begin to see the intention of God and recognize what He desires and how He plans on bringing His desires alive in us so that we may participate with Him in accomplishing those desires. Since most of us want to be happy in life, we set certain goals to be happy, and even if we do not have a list of goals, ultimately, our desire is to be happy. While I believe that God wants us to be happy in life, I do not believe that it is His final and ultimate goal for us. I believe that His ultimate goal for us is to know Him— to really know Him. If we know God the way that He wants us to know Him then it can be said that we are happy because we know where we are going, not just for eternity, but where we are going now. When our lives begin with Christ Jesus on this side of eternity, the plan that Father desired for us all along begins to come into place; however, that plan cannot be fulfilled until we completely release our hearts and minds to Father.

We see in the passage of Romans 12:2 how we are told to be transformed by the renewing of our minds. We cannot simply accept and believe on the Name of Jesus Christ and continue to live the way that we have lived before we accepted and believed that He is our Savior. We have to adopt His mind that we see in Scripture and allow that mindset of God to change the way that we think. We begin by seeing the mercy that God has bestowed upon us in Christ Jesus. We must come to the place where we genuinely see for ourselves what we have been saved from and saved for. Unless we really know that we have been saved from complete and total sin and understand from God what that means, we will not have the conviction to move forward as those who have been saved from sin, instead of those who remain constantly imprisoned by the power of sin. Knowing God intimately and how Jesus Christ has come to save us from sin really does away with the power that sin has held over our minds. While this doesn't mean that we will never sin again while in this world, it does mean that we now have the power, if we truly choose to pursue Christ, to overcome sin by the true knowledge of Him. So my brothers and sisters, it can be said that sin is no longer our greatest problem as believers, but it is the lack of knowing God and His plans for us. Now that we have the power in Christ to renew our minds and think like our elder brother Jesus thinks, we have the ability to know and respond to God the way that He did. There is one major thing that often stands in the way of our total acceptance of Father's will, and that is living under the power of feelings.

We must believe that feelings change. Sometimes it seems as if our feelings change from hour to hour, and if we are honest with ourselves and really think about it, our feelings usually come from what we are thinking. If we believe that God is angry with us, then we are going to try to avoid His presence. If we believe that God is going to keep something from us that we really want in life, then we walk around as children of an angry parent or someone who really doesn't care about certain needs and desires we have. If we feel this way, it is because we are thinking this way. If we are feeling wrong it is because we are thinking wrong.

"For the Lord God is a Sun and Shield; the Lord bestows [present] grace and favor and [future] glory (honor, splendor, and heavenly bliss)! No good thing will He withhold from those who walk uprightly." **PSALM 84:11**

"In my distress [when seemingly closed in] I called upon the Lord and cried to my God; He heard my voice out of His temple (heavenly dwelling place), and my cry came before Him, into His [very] ears." **PSALM 18:6**

"Out of my distress I called upon the Lord; the Lord answered me and set me free and in a large place. The Lord is on my side; I will not fear. What can man do to me?" **PSALM 118:5–6**

These passages that come from God's word are beautiful and true, but to the person who is not willing to accept or believe them, they offer little hope. Unless our minds are changed, being transformed slowly so that we will be able to believe God the way that Romans 12 talks about, able to know what Father's personal will is for us, we will continue to walk under the power of unresolved feelings, feelings that have not been trained by truth. Along with this truth comes an unusual presence of God that brings rest and peace to anchor our sometimes wild and unbridled minds so that we may be able to be still on the inside, regardless of what is going on around us. Two things:

"You will guard him and keep him in perfect and constant peace whose mind [both its inclination and its character] is stayed on You, because he commits himself to You, leans on You, and hopes confidently in You." **ISAIAH 26:3**

"Peace I leave with you; My [own] peace I now give and bequeath to you. Not as the world gives do I give to you. Do not let your hearts be troubled, neither let them be afraid. [Stop allowing yourselves to be agitated and disturbed; and do not permit yourselves to be fearful and intimidated and cowardly and unsettled.]" **JOHN 14:27**

The kind of peace spoken of in these passages is available for everyone who really believes in and on the Name of

Jesus Christ. Jesus mentioned to His disciples, which includes us today, that He was giving us His very own peace. Jesus was not troubled and unstable inwardly as we are, because not only was He the Word of God made flesh, but He was also partaking of human nature, which meant that He had the ability to be at unrest and afraid and lose peace by what He saw around Him. We return to this truth, that Jesus thought like God—He had the thoughts of God in Him, and so do we, if we believe our heavenly Father's words and trust that He personally communicates those words to us through His written word. But I do want to caution us, especially in the arena of hearing and knowing the voice of God—whatever you do, do not limit God and ever think that He is predictable. While we know that our Father's principles are eternal, His method of accomplishing what He desires can very easily change. I have found in my own life that Father changes the way that He executes His will so that He will not become predictable in my life, where the exercising of personal faith is no longer necessary. We have to put our faith into Christ—we have to invest our entire selves into Jesus Christ, if we want to have the powerful presence of peace that He speaks of in His word. As we grow to know that we can have this peace when our feelings are raging with unbelief, worry, and wonder, as to what God is going to do, if anything, when we feel so unsettled. Remember dear ones that our Father's words are eternal, and they can have a powerful effect upon us, if we trust them.

I want to recall to your memory as we close this chapter how we have an enemy—the devil, who is constantly on the prowl, trying to rob us of all the benefits we have in Christ Jesus. One of the most profound ways that Satan does this is by trying

to convince us that God doesn't care about us when we seem to
have insurmountable odds against us, which even seem to contradict His word. But remember dear ones, we are to have an
intimate relationship with Jesus, the Savior, and not the Bible.
The book alone, sitting on a shelf has no redemptive power; however, once the message within is applied to and in our hearts by
faith, we see the power of God operating in it and changing our
lives, enabling us to have what our Father desires for us to have
and when and as He wants us to have it—in His timing. If our
feelings are ever going to stop leading us, we must learn to trust
God's word as He reveals it to us in the Person of Christ. I want
us to notice here that I said the Person of Christ—meaning that
Jesus came as a person Who was and still is capable of speaking
to us, revealing Himself to us, causing the Scriptures to come
alive as a real live Person, Who lives...today!

> *"The secret [of the sweet, satisfying companionship] of the Lord*
> *have they who fear (revere and worship) Him, and He will show*
> *them His covenant and reveal to them its [deep, inner] meaning."*
> **PSALM 25:14**

> *"You search and investigate and pore over the Scriptures diligently*
> *because you suppose and trust that you have eternal life through*
> *them. And these [very Scriptures] testify about Me!"* **JOHN 5:39**

8 —

THE TRYING OF OUR FAITH

"But let endurance and steadfastness and patience have full play and do a thorough work, so that you may be [people] perfectly and fully developed [with no defects], lacking in nothing."
JAMES 1:4

If we are honest with ourselves, we will dogmatically say that no one likes strong discipline. While it is true that we may agree that we like the results of discipline, seldom do we like the work and the difficulty that it takes us to become disciplined. However, we sincerely enjoy the results of a well disciplined life. It can also be said that once we have learned to discipline ourselves in whatever we do, the work of maintaining the lifestyle that discipline offers becomes easier, and as we learn a variety of ways to maintain a good lifestyle, it is much easier not to get in a rut or regimen and become bored with maintaining the way that we enjoy living. The same can be said with developing a strong spiritual life. Have you ever noticed that when there is something you really need to do in life that there seems to be an annoying voice in your head that reminds you that you need to get that thing done that you've been putting off for what seems to be forever? Well, the Holy Spirit does remind and prompt us inwardly that there are certain actions that we need to take in cooperating with Him that bring about spiritual results that are great. Why is it that we need these spiritual disciplines in our lives? Well, for one, when we are disciplined spiritually, our lives are richer, fuller, and we can enjoy God more than when we are not disciplined. So many of us work hard at being better spiritually, but oftentimes we ignore the Holy Spirit, Who is with us to enable us to 'do' the things that our Father wants us to do in life, and as we do the things that our heavenly Father gives us the ability to do, we begin to see how true it is that we are not alone in our labor in this world. Discipline means work, and sometimes very hard work, but if we know that Father is working with us, that the end result is going to be something very special.

> *"[Not in your own strength] for it is God Who is all the while effectually at work in you [energizing and creating in you the power and desire], both to will and to work for His good pleasure and satisfaction and delight."* **PHILIPPIANS 2:13**

> *"We are assured and know that [God being a partner in their labor] all things work together and are [fitting into a plan] for good to and for those who love God and are called according to [His] design and purpose."* **ROMANS 8:28**

So, why then is it so necessary that we become disciplined, and why does discipline and pain have to be so much a part of becoming a strong Christian? The truth is that being disciplined spiritually helps us to have power over the flesh. And our Father uses certain disciplines designed to show us where our weaknesses are in the flesh. Not everyone is tempted by the same thing, but all of us are tempted by something. At any rate, temptation has the power to rule over us and to pull us away from our heavenly Father. And even though He personally disciplines us, we will continue to be tempted in life. But the answer to all of this is not whether we are tempted or not, but what do we do with the temptation when it comes. Remember how we have already talked about the transformation of the mind so that we will know what God's will is and be able to test and prove the will of God through obedience? Likewise, as we grow spiritually through assigned suffering and disciplines from Father, we will begin to recognize His voice more quickly in any circumstance, and be able to go in that direction. Without such discipline, it will be difficult to recognize Father's voice clearly and the leading of His Holy Spirit, and that leads back to quieting the noise that we often have working on the inside. If we are continually controlled by the noise and the influences of what goes on outside of us, it will be very difficult to be able to see how Jesus has already given us peace on the inside that quiets the storms outside. It is for this reason that our faith must be tested. This testing of our faith by God and by what happens to us in this world is intended to bring us to God so that He may show us how to overcome what continues to overcome us. Any noise or any idol in our lives that competes for the love that we have for God must be brought to a place of submission, where we are only led by the Holy Spirit. I want to be sure that we understand that when I say being led by the Holy Spirit, I do not mean giving up the things in life that we enjoy. Our heavenly Father wants us to enjoy what we have in life but does not want what we enjoy in life to master us or have control over us more than His Spirit. We should really understand that when our lives are led along by the Holy Spirit and influenced by Him, it is then that we truly enjoy life and living.

The only way that we can know that we are God's children is through the way that He disciplines us. We can still believe that we are God's children, but a Christian who does not know the discipline of God will constantly try to find that discipline or will wonder why he or she doesn't feel the affirmation that comes from God to those who are His children. If God has accepted and received you as His child, then you will be subjected to discipline. Those of us who do not submit to discipline often find ourselves getting mixed signals from God—does He love me? What do I need to do to please God? Well, the greatest thing that we can do in the beginning is to yield ourselves to God as our Father, even though it may take us sometime to really understand what that means. Since God is our Father, He is quite capable of dealing with us personally, where we already are, and leading us into being mature children of His, who are no longer controlled by what is on the outside. When we become still and quiet on the inside, having been in the disciplined care of our heavenly Father, we realize that God has had some hand in this quiet, because without His leading us into it or parenting us into this quiet through personal discipline, we would not have it in our lives.

"You must submit to and endure [correction] for discipline; God is dealing with you as with sons. For what son is there whom his father does not [thus] train and correct and discipline? Now if you are exempt from correction and left without discipline in which all [of God's children] share, then you are illegitimate offspring and not true sons [at all]." **HEBREWS 12:7-8**

"For the time being no discipline brings joy, but seems grievous and painful; but afterwards it yields a peaceable fruit of righteousness to those who have been trained by it [a harvest of fruit which consists in righteousness—in conformity to God's will in purpose, thought, and action, resulting in right living and right standing with God]." **HEBREWS 12:11**

In my experience with working with many Christians I have often seen that many of us mistake discipline for punishment. I realize that we have been told, especially in working toward improving our physical body through exercise, that we have to punish ourselves until we see the right results. Well, this is self inflicted, but even so, we are still aiming toward a certain goal. If we are to understand the difference between punishment and discipline from God, we simply need to know what motivates God. God is not motivated to get even with us. We see that He has been pleased with the total work of Jesus Christ on the cross, so His motive is not to get even with us as sinners. God's motive in disciplining us is so that we will recognize Him as a Father Who loves us and Who cares that we partake in His holiness as His offspring. If we never learn the difference between punishment and discipline and never submit to this discipline from God, then we will never really know what motivates God and that He truly loves us.

James 1:2–3 tells us this:

"Consider it wholly joyful, my brethren, whenever you are enveloped in or encounter trials of any sort or fall into various temptations. Be assured and understand that the trial and proving of your faith bring out endurance and steadfastness and patience."

We can be absolutely certain that if we are God's children, He will lead us along the pathway of testing, not so that we will be destroyed by those tests, but so that we may overcome them by faith in Him. This disciplined walk is necessary, so that what is outside of us that often tries to rob us of the peace that Jesus has given us begins to lose that power. Tests and trials that we go through with God and not in our own strength, will produce greater Godliness within us so that we may continue to move forward, only to find out, if we continue to walk with God, that we have power to do everything that He has put us in this earth to do as we walk alongside Him.

9 ⎯⎲⎯

WHEN GOD IS SILENT

*"...Unto You do I cry, O Lord my Rock, be not deaf and silent to me, lest, if You be silent to me, I become like those going down to the pit [the grave]. Hear the voice of my supplication as I cry to You for help, as I lift up my hands toward Your innermost sanctuary (the Holy of Holies)." **PSALM 28:1–2***

Perhaps one of the most difficult things to do is to pray and expect God to answer within a certain time frame. When He doesn't, panic sets in. So often we expect God to respond within our time frame or put Him on our clock, when in truth, we are on His clock. Nothing that happens to us ever escapes the eyes of our heavenly Father. He is aware at all times of what is going on in our lives, and if we really understand and accept this, our lives would run so much more smoothly. This does not mean that we will not be challenged or have challenges to deal with in life. No one has a life that is free of challenges, but it is not that we are challenged, but what we do with those challenges when they come that makes the difference.

I often tell the students in our church discipleship school not to put Father in a box and how it is necessary to have a foundation with God. This means that it is good to start out our relationship with Father, allowing Him to speak most of the time. If we will learn to do this and cultivate it well, it will be to our greater benefit. One of the reasons why it is good to have this kind of track-record or foundation with God is because then we have something to fall back on; not because God will fail us, but because our memories often fail and we cannot remember exactly what Father has told us. The truly experienced sons or daughters of God who train themselves to really listen to God and to wait in His Presence, are able to know when Father is about to do something. In other words, our human spirits can be trained to recognize when God is about to do what He has said to us. When the Lord is silent or quiet this doesn't mean that He has taken a disinterest in what we are going through. He is simply allowing time to pass as it always does and the passing of time is what often tests what we believe about God. Do we really believe that God has spoken to us?

> "...[Even the migratory birds are punctual to their seasons.] Yes, the stork [excelling in the great height of her flight] in the heavens knows her appointed times of [migration], and the turtledove, the swallow, and the crane observe the time of their return. But My people do not know the law of the Lord [which the lower animals instinctively recognize in so far as it applies to them]."
> **JEREMIAH 8:7**

If we are really going to take advantage of the waiting periods that Father allows all of us to go through, then we must begin to recognize the times and seasons by which He does things. The son or daughter who busies himself during the times when Father is silent usually meditates upon what Father has spoken before the period of silence. Can you remember what Father has spoken to you during the times when He is quiet? Do you fall back upon His words when you feel bad, discouraged, disappointed, and wondering if you did not hear Father correctly? Surely, the Father always tells us what He is going to do several times because we are very hard of hearing at times. When our Father is speaking to us about what He wants to do we often do not hear Him clearly because we are focused on what we would like for Him to do. It is essential that we learn to rely on Father's faithfulness. The more we develop a listening ear when He *is* speaking to us, the more powerful we'll be able to stand when He *isn't*. Everything that our Father tells us will eventually be put to the test. Since He already knows what we are going to do, He allows what is in us to be put to the test, so that we will be able to see that He is genuinely faithful at the end. This visibility of God's faithfulness in the end will also strengthen us and keep us strong so that we will know that our Father has truly spoken. Sadly, many of us give up when difficulties arise in our lives. We forget what Father has spoken and believe that the obvious trials and difficulties that we are going through are a sign that we didn't hear God correctly. Never believe that when God speaks that everything will run smoothly. Yes, it can run smoothly—surely, it can; however, this kind of smooth sailing doesn't happen until later in our walk with God when our faith is truly solidified in Him, and no matter what happens we remain strong, because we've grown to trust God's faithfulness when He is quiet.

When we are walking through a time period when Father isn't speaking or is not addressing the difficulties we believe He should be addressing in our lives, He is well aware of where we are and eventually, in the outcome, we will see this for ourselves. Everyone I know welcomes good news. When God speaks a very encouraging word, everyone rejoices; however, I have learned that when Father speaks a word, He is talking about what which is forthcoming. We are often so bound in the present that we fail to understand that when Father reveals to us what is going to happen that there is a transitional period through which we go from one place to the other, often not realizing that difficulty awaits us as we walk through that open door of transition. It is key that we remember what Father has told us specifically. The enemy will come and try his best to rob us of what Father has spoken, and he will use the bad circumstances that we are going through to make us feel as if Father has not spoken to us. Too many times we give in to what the circumstances tell us rather than believe what Father has spoken to us. However, the one who truly holds on and believes God, declaring what Father has spoken in the circumstances is the person who receives what Father has spoken. It is very possible to disobey God in difficult situations and thus completely abort and miss out on what Father has promised. Be careful not to allow your hearts to harden during difficulties. So many times we feel that Father has left us or is punishing us when difficulties come, but we can learn that these difficulties train us to be stronger by putting to death the nature of the flesh's control over our spirits. What we consider punishment is very often the discipline that Father uses to make us more spiritually sound, so that the flesh no longer tells us what to do.

> *"...So, since Christ suffered in the flesh for us, for you, arm yourselves with the same thought and purpose [patiently to suffer rather than fail to please God]. For whoever has suffered in the flesh [having the mind of Christ' is done with [intentional] sin [has stopped pleasing himself and the world, and pleases God]. So that he can no longer spend the rest of his natural life living by [his human appetites and desires, but [he lives] for what God wills."* **1 PETER 5:1–2**

There is much power that comes when we respond to God the right way in difficulty and when He is silent. Remember what Father has spoken to you just before His voice goes silent—He has nothing new to tell you or anything different to say; use the word that He has given you to establish a firmer grip during what seems to be difficult times. The word that Father gives us is a weapon against what will come against us when circumstances contradict what He says. Remember that Father is indeed the Author and Perfecter of our faith and is able to over ride any circumstance that says otherwise. He is famous for doing the impossible, and will do the impossible for those who depend on Him and remain steadfast in their faith even when He is silent.

Now, one more passage of Scripture before we close this chapter.

> *"...Give attention to this! Behold, a sower went out to sow. And as he was sowing, some seed fell along the path, and the birds came and ate it up. Other seed [of the same kind] fell on ground*

full of rocks, where it had not much soil; and at once it sprang up, because it had no depth of soil; And when the sun came up, it was scorched, and because it had not taken root, it withered away. Other seed [of the same kind] fell among thorn plants, and the thistles grew and pressed together and utterly choked and suffocated it, and it yielded no grain. And other seed [of the same kind] fell into good (well-adapted) soil and brought forth grain, growing up and increasing, and yielded up to thirty times as much, and sixty times as much, and even a hundred times as much as had been sown..." MARK 4:3–8

"...The sower sows the Word. The ones along the path are those who have the Word sown [in their hearts], but when they hear, Satan comes at once and [by force] takes away the message which is sown in them. And in the same way the ones sown upon stony ground are those who, when they hear the Word, at once receive and accept and welcome it with joy; And they have no real root in themselves, and so they endure for a little while; then when trouble or persecution arises on account of the Word, they immediately are offended (become displeased, indignant, resentful) and they stumble and fall away. And the ones sown among the thorns are others who hear the Word; Then the cares and anxieties of the world and distractions of the age, and the pleasure and delight and false glamour and deceitfulness of riches, and the craving and passionate desire for other things creep in and choke and suffocate the Word, and it becomes fruitless. And those sown on the good (well-adapted) soil are the ones who hear the Word and receive and accept and welcome it and bear fruit—some thirty times as much as was sown, some sixty times as much, and some [even] a hundred times as much." MARK 4:14–20

A good question that we can ask ourselves here is: 'What kind of soil am I? What is my response to what Father says as far as His spoken words to me carried out in my life? It takes time for the Word of God to bring forth fruit in our lives. As we see here in this parable of the sower that Jesus shared, our Father is always sharing and sowing His Word, but we are not always recipients of His word until the actual end. When our Father is quiet, it does not mean that nothing is going on, much like during the winter when snow has covered the earth. Although we do not see the fresh green leaves of spring, something is happening underneath the ground that is preparing the tree for what is to come. Much like this experience, when Father speaks to us, we may not see anything at all. We may only know difficulty for a while, and Father is silent, but just because He is silent doesn't mean that nothing is going on. Remember that when Father is quiet, use His silence to speak to you loudly as you go through difficulty, as we all do.

⌁ 10

REST COMES WITH BEING STILL

No one who has been born again wants to continue sinning. The truth is that the more we grow to know God as our Father, the less we do sin and the more conscious we are of the new nature—the nature that we have inherited from God. It is impossible to enjoy God the way that we are supposed to enjoy Him if there is a conflict of interest in our hearts—that is, if we do not know what Jesus Christ has done for us on the cross, we cannot really enjoy being with God. Even as believers we will sin from time to time, but we must understand that it doesn't mean that we have lost our salvation just because we sin once we have known Christ. The key to successfully walking with God in our new nature or being new creatures, is to completely accept the truth about ourselves as we now are. The more we know the truth and practice it, the more aware we become of the power that we now have over Satan and the defeated lifestyle we have lived up to this point.

"...Therefore if any person is [ingrafted] in Christ (the Messiah) he is a new creation (a new creature altogether); the old [previous moral and spiritual condition] has passed away. Behold, the fresh and new has come!" **2 CORINTHIANS 5:17**

"...We know [absolutely] that anyone born of God does not [deliberately and knowingly] practice committing sin, but the One Who was begotten of God carefully watches over and protects him [Christ's divine presence within him preserves him against the evil], and the wicked one does not lay hold (get a grip) on him or touch [him]." **1 JOHN 5:18**

"...If we [freely] admit that we have sinned and confess our sins, He is faithful and just (true to His own nature and promises) and will forgive our sins [dismiss our lawlessness] and [continuously] cleanse us from all unrighteousness [everything not in conformity to His will in purpose, thought, and action]." **1 JOHN 1:9**

It can sometimes be very difficult for us when we sin against God. We can feel the hurt within us that our Father has always felt regarding our sin nature and how it separated us. However, the good news is that we are now able to confess this sin to the Father and move on with our lives. This does not mean that we have been given a license to sin, but rather, we have been given the power in believing in Jesus' Name to overcome what sin had done to us up until we accepted the truth about Jesus Christ in the Scriptures. We must remember that the same Spirit Who has revealed Jesus to us so that we might be saved, continues to reveal the truth about God now that we are saved. The Holy

Spirit keeps us in the truth, and even though the truth of our heavenly Father is simple, it can be very profound, especially in the arena where our sins are concerned.

I remember not long ago I sinned against Father—at least, I felt that I had sinned against Him. The first thing that I do when I feel as if I have sinned against God is to ask for forgiveness. I ask for forgiveness because I can tell that my intimacy is restored to God immediately; that is, if I believe and accept what God says about Himself and myself regarding sin. If I confess my sin then He is faithful and just to forgive me of my sin and cleanse me from all unrighteousness. This is the truth. It is true whether I believe it or not, but it doesn't work for me unless I believe and accept it within my own heart. It is through this acceptance of the truth that I walk in the reality of what the truth says, and so it is with all of us. The more we believe what Father tells us, the more we are given the opportunity to see the truth of it in reality.

As I mulled over feeling bad for my sin, the Lord spoke to my heart, saying: "Do you think you can come up with a better plan than I've already given regarding your sin?" And for a moment I thought about what He said. Before He spoke to me I was thinking about my sin and how badly I felt and whether there was something I could do to feel better about myself. But there is no truth given other than what Father has given us in Jesus Christ that will not only make us feel better, but also make us feel (right) with God, which is what we are looking for anyway. We believe that when we are feeling badly that we want to feel good; but in truth, the feeling that we are looking for is to be restored to feeling or being 'right' with God. This can only come by being obedient to what He has already told us. Believing God carries with it the power to enter into a restful life that Father wants all of us to enjoy. God doesn't choose one person to rest, but He is looking for all of us to know Him intimately through His Word and to believe Him so that what has controlled us up to this point in our lives will lose its power over us.

God wants us to enjoy a certain quietness. He wants us to be familiar with it, and in that quietness we will become familiar with the way He speaks and addresses us. As we grow to know that Father is with us in every situation, no matter what that situation is, we will grow to know more of what He is like and what we are like as His dear children. It is true that Father will allow certain circumstances or conditions to come into our lives that are well beyond our ability to control. As we cry out to Him, He will ultimately draw us to Himself. Of course, I realize that we are naturally independent, and this state of independency has gotten us into trouble because it often leads us away from the very best that God has to offer. We must remember that Satan caused Adam and Eve to believe that Father was keeping something from them. Let us be encouraged to know that whatever Father may keep from us He will replace with something better!

If we were to look at this a bit more naturally, we can see the resemblance between our growing up spiritually to recognize God and to walk in rest and quiet with Him and a child who is being weaned. The child is restless because the bottle has been taken from him, and while the pacifier may reduce the fretting to some degree, the child still whines for the bottle. This is what he has known for quite some time, and letting go is difficult. We grow up in Christ by Father taking us away from the familiar, and leading us into unfamiliar territory. The new territory that our Father leads us into will often provide the challenges that will cause us to become more intimate with Him. We are usually aware of the fact that God is with us in our minds, but to see God working on our behalf in our everyday lives, reveals that He is truly with us. Father will lead us into difficult situations, so that we may experience Him working in them. So many of us fail when difficulty comes and we sometimes accuse God of not being good or not being with us in stressful situations or those that challenge us to grow stronger.

"...Surely I have calmed and quieted my soul; like a weaned child with his mother, like a weaned child is my soul within me [ceased from fretting]." **PSALM 131:2**

And just as it is with a weaned child, once we know that God is with us in the difficulties of life, we cease fretting as well. The more our minds see that God is truthful to His Word, the more quiet we are on the inside and the more we begin to see from a different perspective. The difficulties that we face and endure in this world should all lead us to a more intimate relationship with Jesus Christ, and the more intimate we become with Him, the less we will be tossed to and fro by what happens to us in this world.

One way that we can check to see if we are becoming more quiet within is to see how we respond when something difficult or out of our control occurs. When we respond in peace and consider the Lord first or shortly after the situation, we are moving toward realizing that Father is indeed the One Who is able to cause us to have peace and rest. This leads us to being still on the inside no matter what happens to us outwardly.

11

OUR MINDS ARE CHANGED WHEN WE ARE STILL

*"...You will guard him and keep him in perfect and constant peace whose mind [both its inclination and its character] is stayed on You, because he commits himself to You, leans on You, and hopes confidently in You." **ISAIAH 26:3***

*"Great peace have they who love Your law; nothing shall offend them or make them stumble." **PSALM 119:165***

I think that it would be very safe to say that most of us worry about what is going to happen, even when Father tells us or gives us some insight into the future. One of the responsibilities of the Holy Spirit is to reveal to us what our Father is planning in the future. While He will never give us all the details all at once, He will prepare us for what is to come, if we are willing to listen. One of the greatest enemies of being able to be still before Father is impatience. We are in a society where everything is hurried and even though we can cause things to be done with the push of a button, we are no more patient now than we were before. What we should recognize and hold to heart is that no matter how fast technology may push us, our heavenly Father will never be hurried to get things done. God doesn't change and because He does not change, we can rely on Him to do exactly what He says and exactly when He chooses to do so.

The more we recognize that Father doesn't change, the more we will find peace in whatever He has planned for us. Father will use disturbing circumstances so that we will seek our way to Him and emerge from the prison of worry where we often find ourselves.

The truth of the matter is no one likes to wait—at least not for very long. Sometimes we get confused between waiting on the Lord and waiting for what we would like the Lord to do for us, or what we want from God. There is a difference. If our attention is focused on something from God it becomes more difficult to wait for that thing to come to us. Our focus is on the thing rather than the One Who is able to give the thing to us. Our primary aim as Christians should be to know God, not to simply pray and get things from God. Many of us have been taught that God is in heaven and we should pray to get things from Him or pray that our lives will be better or easier in this earth. Our lives may not be easy, but we can have power over what controls humanity, that is, if we have faith in Christ.

"...Do not therefore, fling away your fearless confidence, for it carries a great and glorious compensation of reward. For you have need of steadfast patience and endurance, so that you may perform and fully accomplish the will of God, and thus receive

*and carry away [and enjoy to the full] what is promised. For still
a little while (a very little while), and the Coming One will come
and He will not delay."* **HEBREWS 10:36–37**

We have to wait. We must learn to wait on God and to
believe that His plans are good for us; however, if we continue
to run away from the plan of God and try to manage our lives,
then we will continue to live with frustration. Father wants us to
have peace just as the opening Scripture says, but that peace will
come when we allow our souls to rely on Father's truth and not
on what we want our Father to hurry and do for us. Peace comes
when our minds are settled. Peace comes when we are still and
quiet in Father's presence, allowing Him to speak to us so that we
may know His calendar and timetable for our lives.

This is what we are told in Romans:

*"...Do not be conformed to this world (this age), [fashioned
after and adapted to its external, superficial customs], but be
transformed (changed) by the [entire] renewal of your mind
[by its new ideals and its attitude], so that you may prove [for
yourselves] what is the good and acceptable and perfect will of
God, even the thing which is good and acceptable and perfect [in
His sight for you]."* **ROMANS 12:2**

Oftentimes we think that Father doesn't want us to have any
choice about what happens in our lives; but in truth, our heavenly
Father wants us to know that we are co-laborers alongside Him.
Even though this is the truth, Father still knows the road that He
has chosen for us to follow, and in order for us to successfully

find and maintain our lives with and in Christ, we have to honor and obey Father. In the beginning stages of learning to know and walk with Father, our lives may seem a bit mechanical, but that is because we have never really known what it means to live a disciplined life. Yes, to be disciplined does mean that we have certain restrictions. However, the more we obey Father's instructions that bring discipline, the more we clearly see that they are freeing, giving us the freedom that Father desires so that we may enjoy life, each other, and especially our walk with God. Father's speech is that of truth and authority, so He knows exactly what He means and is never mistaken. As we grow to know this unmistakable voice better, our minds are settled and the rat race that often commands our attention in this world begins to settle and we are no longer drawn so easily by it.

> *"...The Lord is my Shepherd [to feed, guide, and shield me], I shall not lack....He refreshes and restores my life (my self); He leads me in the paths of righteousness [uprightness and right standing with Him—not for my earning it, but] for His name's sake."* **PSALM 23:1,3**

During the course of time as we surrender ourselves more and more to Father, it will be because we are falling more in love with Him. As we fall in love with Father, we will begin to understand and accept His lead. This happens because we are growing to know that Father's only motivation toward us is love. Because of Satan's DNA, which was implanted within all mankind back in the Garden of Eden, we are afraid to trust. Deception always breeds mistrust, so much of our relating with God in the beginning will have to do with our struggle to trust Him. This is because we have not yet grown to know or recognize Him, and if we do not know Father, we will never know that His motivation for wanting to be intimate has to do with His great love for us.

Obedience to God will soon cause us to know that He is with us. This is true because the more we are able to obey what we are told by the Holy Spirit, the more we will have peace, and the more we have peace, the less our minds will struggle with what Father is sharing with us and doing in our lives. The more that we are able to walk with Father in this manner, quiet on the inside and able to hear Him inwardly no matter what is going on around us, the more capable we are to build the kingdom alongside Him and to rest quietly in His leadership.

Again, this kind of walking with Father takes time; however, it is not impossible but quite doable. We simply have to recognize our constant need for Father, no matter how many prayers have been answered or how many miracles we may have seen. Our constant reliance upon God will continue to afford us the strength and power that we need in following Him into the life that He has called us to live.

> *"...For we are God's [own] handiwork (His workmanship), recreated in Christ Jesus, [born anew] that we may do those good works which God predestined (planned beforehand) for us [taking paths which He prepared ahead of time], that we should walk in them [living the good life which He prearranged and made ready for us to live]." **EPHESIANS 2:10***

Sometimes much of our restlessness and inability to be still inwardly is because we simply do not know what Father wants from us or what He wants us to do. Because Father knew what He created us for and what He desires for us to do, it would be wise to consider this and to go to Him, asking Him for wisdom and insight into His plan. Such a prayer goes well with Father because He knows that sometimes in our non-spiritual approach, we cannot discover or know what His plans are for us. However, the good news is that Father wants to share that wisdom with us. He wants to tell us what He has created us to do so that we may move in that direction, having clear minds and a fresh silence that has now come into our hearts because we have indeed heard from God.

> *"...Because He has inclined His ear to me, therefore will I call upon Him as long as I live.....Return to your rest, O my soul, for the Lord has dealt bountifully with you."* **PSALM 116:2,7**

For the most part, all we need to know is that God is indeed for us—He is not our enemy. He is not the One keeping us from succeeding. He is simply waiting for us to stop trying to succeed without Him. For before we were born, He knew us even then, and was excited about the plans that He had for us. All we need do is come into His presence and be still, wait, and listen, so that He may reveal those plans to us and then walk with us in carrying them out. Until our minds are being changed by the thoughts of our heavenly Father, we will continue to be in somewhat of a combative relationship with Him, not really knowing what He wants and hearing what seems to be mixed messages from Father. However, as we move forward, giving up our lives to Father, which can be painfully difficult, He meets us and allows us to know that He understands difficulty. We see this in the life of Jesus Christ, and just as Father walked with Jesus, He also walks with us.

~~12

SIN CAUSES RESTLESSNESS

"...If I regard iniquity in my heart, the Lord will not hear me..."
PSALM 66:18

I am sometimes amazed and surprised at how many Christians would like to think that God negotiates with us concerning sinful behavior or sinful attitudes. So many of us would like to think that God takes sides with us when we have been offended or hurt by someone else, and especially by other Christians. It can be difficult to be offended and hurt by someone, the important thing is not that we are offended, but it is what we do with the offense when it occurs. Oftentimes when someone hurts me, I rationalize why it happened, try to understand why it happened, and wonder why the person did it. I cannot simply excuse the behavior, and I do not believe any of us do, because that is what makes an offense an offense, it hurts us and pulls us into an emotional way of thinking, rather than a spiritual way of thinking, where Father is able to influence our thoughts.

It is very important to understand and to accept the truth that whenever someone sins against us, we should never turn inward and try to rationalize what we should do about it. Whenever we turn inward, listening to the sometimes very loud voice of 'self,' the end result is something that we do in the flesh rather than what the Spirit of God would have us do. So how do we avoid further harm when we are offended?

The best way to deal with an offense is to acknowledge that none of us have consistently perfect behavior, no matter how mature we may be as Christians. We have mood swings from time to time and difficulties in this world that may challenge the Spirit of God at work within; and when this happens, we can act very rudely and be ugly toward each other. The best way to remedy and to maintain healthy relationships is to deal with offenses quickly, even when we may not be completely ready to do so. This means that when someone has harmed or hurt us, we should let them know as soon as we can, and without accusation. Let us remember that offenses hurt badly because we take them personally, whether or not they are intended to be personal. Many of us can wear our feelings on our sleeves even unknowingly, and when someone says something or does something that seems cross, we immediately take offense to it. An offense, if not dealt with properly, will always become something worse. No offense, depending on how bad it is, remains at the same level as when we were first offended. As we hold on to it and nurse it, it becomes something far worse, and the hurt becomes a deep wound. Bear in mind that a wound is deeper than a hurt and harder to deal with. The longer we nurse our hurts and find fault with those who have harmed us, the deeper the hurt goes and becomes a wound that often carries bitterness, anger, and resentment with it. This is not an easy place to come back from, so we should be careful that our pride does not cause us to hold on to an offense any longer than we should. The best way to handle an offense is never to take it so personally. As strong and maturing Christians, we will continue to be offended, but the more we yield our souls to the influence of the Holy Spirit, the more quickly we'll know how to handle the offense. Truth be told, we'll spend a lot less time asking for forgiveness for offending others and going to others who have offended us. It should be recognized and understood that all of us are capable of offending someone—none of us are exempt, but we should also understand that we should not intentionally offend someone to harm them. The Holy Spirit has a unique way of showing us sin from His perspective, and when He does, He shows us in such a way that we are convicted and convinced of our sin, but never condemned by what the Holy Spirit shows us if we obey what He shares. But if we disagree with the Holy Spirit, we will disobey what He reveals to us, especially when we have been hurt by someone else, the sin (often defined by the hurt we feel) remains. It doesn't just go away with time, but it remains.

Our opening Scripture mentions regarding iniquity in our hearts. To regard iniquity in our hearts means to hold on to it, to have regards to what has happened to us far greater than the Holy Spirit's ability to reason with us. One of the ways we loosen the hold of sin in our hearts is to praise God. We do not praise God for the offense that causes us to regard sin in our hearts, but we praise Him for the power that comes from Him that loosens sins power over us so that we may get past the offense.

God never agrees with us when we are in sin. He never shows favoritism toward any Christian, no matter how much we may think He loves us and cares for us. Wrong is wrong, and the Holy Spirit will always show you where you are wrong, and how to bring peace in a good relationship gone bad. It is good to understand that our goal should always be to make peace however we can—not to find fault and continue the hurts that are often begun with offenses that we've allowed to become more personal than they should, causing hurts that become deep wounds. Forgive quickly. Get past the point of sin and rationalizing as soon as possible. Come out of agreement with sin and begin to seek the influence, love, and truth that come from the Holy Spirit, Who hates division and strife between Believers.

If we are going to learn how to rest, to be still inside, where there is silence, and the power of the Holy Spirit working within us, changing us, causing us to love the way He loves, then we must get to the place where we do not regard sin of any kind in our hearts. Too often we think about how bad our sins are, but this usually happens because we do not know how great our God is from experience with Him. Dear children, the more we walk with our God as He leads us, the more we dwell in His power. We do not continue to act like babies who walk with our feelings and emotions on our sleeves, practically waiting for someone to hurt us so that we may continue sipping from our spiritual bottles. A maturing Christian focuses on the power and nature of Jesus Christ, and not what someone else does to him.

When our hearts are not in tune with the Spirit of our Father, we are not at rest. And when we are not at rest, we are not able to be still before God. An example of this in my own personal walk is when I come in to pray and cannot focus because of some distraction or something that is prevalent on my heart that keeps me from becoming still before God, so that He may speak to me and cause my heart to be quiet and still. Our souls are often troubled when we come before God, our busyness from life itself is often a distraction and a robber of the rest that Father desires for us to have in His presence as we are still and quiet before Him. It is when we are able to be still and quiet before Father that He is able to speak and give us insight and instruction, should He need to, so that our hearts may remain quiet, no matter what tries to get inside our spirits and rob us of our Father's peace.

> "...And the effect of righteousness will be peace [internal and external], and the result of righteousness will be quietness and confident trust forever. My people shall dwell in a peaceable habitation, in safe dwellings, and in quiet resting-places."
> **ISAIAH 31:17–18**

Oftentimes we would like to believe that we will never have this kind of peace that our Father is speaking about until we are in heaven with Him; but truth be told, as Christians, we are already in our Father's kingdom. The peace that we have comes from Jesus Christ—it is His very own peace, and it is not based upon the cooperation of others for us to keep it. It comes from our Father Who has given it to us so that we may live quietly in this world. I am speaking of a heart peace, that when it is mature, stands as a guard against those things which try to rob us of the quiet, peace, and stillness that has been given to us by Father. My dear ones, if we are going to walk in this kind of peace, we must guard ourselves against taking up offenses, and offering excuses as to why we are holding them. No act of injustice to any of us justifies us taking offense, losing our peace and possibly dying earlier than Father plans. Believe me when I tell you this, the bitterness, anger, hatred, depression, discouragement, and a host of other ailments that come from offenses will destroy and eventually kill the human body.

I opened this chapter talking about the harmful effects of holding on to offenses because this is a major problem for Christians. Our Father has given us a way out of the power of sin that comes with holding on to what others have done to us. Forgiveness is an extraordinarily powerful tool against the work of Satan when it comes to being offended. Satan wants us to be un-rested. He wants us to insist that those who have harmed us come back and make it right. Obviously, when we are hurt or offended by someone we begin to feel the need for justice, but hear me again as we close out this chapter. Justice comes not from what that person may or may not do, but it comes from the shed blood of Jesus Christ on the cross, and the shedding of the blood is just as powerful today as it was then, offering power and reconciliation for all sin! However, unless we are willing to forgive the trespasses of others and the harm that they have done to us, we will never be able to get past the horrible enslavement of being offended. No matter how much we pray or think about it, we must obey the word of God concerning being offended. We can forgive what someone has done to us by coming into agreement with the Holy Spirit Who wants to give us comfort from offenses, but this will not and cannot happen if we do not agree with Him and see sin from His perspective. Until we see what sin has done to all of us from the perspective of our dear Savior, we will continue to look for justice elsewhere; my dear friends—there is *none* elsewhere.

> *"...Return to your rest, O my soul, for the Lord has dealt bountifully with you."* **PSALM 116:7**

13 —↲—
LIVING IN DENIAL

"...Come to terms quickly with your accuser while you are on the way traveling with him, lest your accuser hand you over to the judge, and the judge to the guard, and you be put in prison."
MATTHEW 5:25

None of us like being wrong. There is something about having the right answer at just the right time that seems to do wonders for your self-esteem, but even so, we are not always right and there are times when we need to be corrected. Nothing is wrong with being corrected. We can learn some very valuable things about having such a submitted and humble spirit where others can speak into our lives, regardless of where we may be in our spiritual walk with Jesus. The important thing to know is that as long as we are alive, we can be taught something of value, even from someone who may not be as mature as we are. It is true that wisdom comes from getting older, but what is more important is that the wisdom that we acquire with age causes us to be more helpful to the forthcoming generation. I often share with younger Believers that the Gospel message is one size fits all. The problem is that we all come from varying backgrounds, where difficulty has affected us in different ways, so we have to adjust and yield our behaviors to the Gospel itself rather than according to how we feel. Because the Gospel message doesn't change, we can also know that the message Author does not change. Our heavenly Father doesn't need to change because He is perfect and flawless in all His ways, but we need to be changed and transformed back to our original design, as Father created us, so that we can live peacefully and quietly from within with Him, just as He intended. But in order to do this, we must recognize and deal with the things that try to hurt and harm us. They will not go away on their own, so we have to overcome them by living in and growing in the faith that our Father has already imparted to us. Our faith level is not intended to stay in the same place. Just as we grow physically, our heavenly Father desires that our level of faith grows even as we grow physically. Now, how is this done, this growing of our faith level? Our faith grows by accepting what Father speaks to us naturally. And nothing is wrong with asking questions when we do not understand certain things that Father speaks to us, but we cannot expect to contend with God and come out on the other end as righteous, unless we agree with Him. Agreeing with God and coming into conformance with the life style that He has chosen for us always produces good fruit in our lives. The kind of fruit that I am speaking about is a more natural desire to love God and to desire to love others as well. Intimacy with God will always produce a deeper love for Him, for our-self, and for others also. If we are to see sin from the perspective of how it has hurt and destroyed so many, then we must see it from Father's perspective and what He has done about sin through the death, burial, and resurrection of Jesus Christ, His First-born son. God hates sin for what it does to people, and if we are going to really understand how sin hurts us, we must admit to sin if it is actively present in our lives and learn how to master it. Most of us do not like the presence of sin in our lives—none of us should—but when we recognize that sin is active in our lives by the revelation of the Holy Spirit, it is wise to come into agreement with the Holy Spirit concerning that sin. When I say come into agreement with the Holy Spirit, I mean to recognize and admit the sin itself as far as committing it, and to confess that the sin is actively harming us and others around us. A sinful lifestyle affects people. Others who are closely associated with us will feel the result of what sin is doing in our lives, so we must come into agreement with what sin is doing, so that the Holy Spirit is able to expel sin's power. How is this done?

Recently, I was speaking to a friend over the phone who was being tormented by fear. So much so that he was finding it hard to make the next move in his life where God was leading him. In such a case where fear is debilitating, it is not the time to live in denial by saying, 'I am not afraid,' and feigning faith. The wise thing to do here is to admit before God and in our own hearts that we are terrified and that this fear is tormenting us and keeping us from moving ahead with God. Faith and tormenting fear will never co-exist—they serve different purposes. Faith is intended to reveal the way of Christ and the work of God in our lives and it works for the past and the future at the same time.

In other words, when we are living by faith, God is able to reveal to us what He has done in the past, up until the present moment, so that we may move forward, even if the circumstances tell us otherwise. Where there are great mountains in the way of what seems to be our spiritual progress, the Father is able to move those as we travel more forward, causing what is not seen to become visible by our operating in faith. The opposite occurs when we live in fear. Fear steals vision. It kills the progress that Father desires for us to make as His children. Faith and fear may be present at the same time, but only one can win. Whichever one wins is determined by which one we give the most power to. It is when we come into agreement with our adversary, and in this case, it would be fear, that we begin to gain power over it.

If we continue to deny that we have fear when clearly it is present like it was in my friend's heart, then we have no power from God to get rid of it; however, as we acknowledge it and its power over us to lead us to sin, then we can come into agreement with the power of God which brings faith, and this fear is dispelled.

An example of what to do would be to pray this way: "Father, I am terribly afraid. Terribly. In fact, I am so afraid that I cannot think, and I'm finding it hard to breathe. But Father, I am reminded of what you have done for me and what you have told me. As I remember in Scripture, the Israelites were met with giants in the Promised Land who caused them to be afraid, but you had already conquered their greatest enemy up to that point, in Egypt. Father, as I am trembling here in fear, agreeing with the fact that I am afraid, please help me to regain my spiritual focus and footing and remember how you have been with me all along and helped me from the beginning up until now."

This is what it means to come into agreement with your adversary. When we come into agreement with the fact that whatever is bothering us and robbing us of faith, it weakens the power of the adversary over us. To admit that we are having a problem doesn't make us less spiritual; it opens up the doorway so that we may receive power to overcome whatever is overcoming us.

When I explained this to my good friend, he began to see the truth in the matter and even as we ended our conversation, peace was beginning to take the place of this tormenting fear so that he could move forward. Dear ones, let us remember what I've often shared and that is to have an established faith track record with God. As we walk with Father, we will always have something to fall back on. There is nothing greater than having Father to fall back on and rest upon when we run into spiritual snags or those things that try to hinder and stop us from reaching our destined spiritual goals.

⌁ 14

LEARNING TO TALK TO GOD

"...Confess to one another therefore your faults (your slips, your false steps, your offenses, your sins) and pray [also] for one another, that you may be healed and restored [to a spiritual tone of mind and heart]." **JAMES 5:16**

onfession plays a very powerful role in the way that we live as overcomers in Christ. It can also be one of the most difficult things for us to do, because many of us often believe that if people knew the secrets we have or sins that we may struggle with, they wouldn't like us any more. Confession has a powerful affect in our lives when we confess to the right person or people. It enables us to keep sin at a very minimal place in our lives, but it also teaches us to approach our heavenly Father as well as each other from a very humble position. Pride is always the enemy of humility, where humility sets us up with a very powerful audience with Father. Confession is a means by which we keep ourselves humble and maintain a clear conscience before God, but it also opens the door so that our conversations with God become easier. Many of us have been taught that our prayers or talking to our heavenly Father should be closely limited to telling Him what we need and asking for His blessings upon certain things and people. However, our heavenly Father desires for His communication with us to be far more than this, and confession plays a very large part in the open communication line that we already have with God because of Jesus Christ His Son. It is when we are not willing to confess our sins and faults that communing with Father becomes strained and difficult. We must remember that confession is for us. It is not for God. Our heavenly Father already knows what we have done, and has given us a way to be released from the power of sin through Jesus Christ our Lord, but unless we embrace His great sacrifice, our communication with Him remains unclear and uncertain at best. The more we keep a clear conscience before Father and before our brothers and sisters, the easier it will be for Father to communicate His love to us however He chooses.

> "...When I kept silence [before I confessed], my bones wasted away through my groaning all the day long. For day and night Your hand [of displeasure] was heavy upon me; my moisture was turned into the drought of summer...I acknowledged my sin to You, and my iniquity I did not hide, I said, I will confess my transgressions to the Lord [continually unfolding the past till all is told]—then You [instantly] forgave me the guilt and iniquity of my sin." *PSALM 32:3, 4A, 5*

"...If we [freely] admit that we have sinned and confess our sins, He is faithful and just (true to His own nature and promises) and will forgive our sins [dismiss our lawlessness] and [continuously] cleanse us from all unrighteousness [everything not in conformity to His will in purpose, thought, and action." **1 JOHN 1:9**

Confession for us must be complete. We must simply empty our hearts before Father or each other as the Holy Spirit gives us instruction. This kind of openness toward God and toward one another robs Satan of his ability to accuse us of wrong doing. Sadly, many of us defend our right to be right rather than doing what it takes to restore peace between others and ourselves. One of the ways that confession keeps our ability to communicate with Father open is that it helps to keep our conscience clear, and if our conscience is clear then we are not afraid to share our hearts with Father.

The clearer our conscience is before God, the easier it is to hear His voice, to recognize it more quickly, and be able to follow His instructions as He gives them. Being able to hear from God in such a clear way gives rest to our hearts, giving us yet another way to rest in Father's presence. If we really love Father then we should want to hear His voice clearly, not only to hear God talk to us, but to commune with Him on a very intimate level. This can happen only when we do as He instructs, especially in the areas where we often struggle with keeping peace and having intimate fellowship with our brothers and sisters. It is wise to remember that as soon as we may feel offended by our brother and sister for something that they've done, we should be willing (if we have to) to go to them and make it right immediately. I said "if" because

as we grow up in our faith we will not become offended as easily
nor be as touchy as we were when were growing up from being
baby Believers.

⌇~ 15

IN TIMES OF STRUGGLE

*"...Do not, therefore, fling away your fearless confidence, for it carries a great and glorious compensation of reward. For you have need of steadfast patience and endurance, so that you may perform and fully accomplish the will of God, and thus receive and carry away [and enjoy to the full] what is promised. For still a little while (a very little while), and the Coming One will come and He will not delay. But the just shall live by faith..." **HEBREWS 10:35–38A***

Everyone who lives for God and tries to walk with Him and do His will comes into difficulty—sometimes what seems to be insurmountable difficulty, and we have no ability to do anything to change it. God ordains difficulty for each of us in His own way. Many times I have seen well meaning Christians go through difficulty and allow the difficulty to cloud their view of God, and have often fallen away from God because of the difficulty. My dear friends, adversity causes us to rise above what

happens to us in this world. Christians are not exempt from adversity, but should find God in it. But to find God in it, we must
believe that He is there and look for Him in it. One of my favorite
passages of Scripture has to do with Hagar being put out of the
camp of Abraham and Sarah. The sad thing is that Hagar was a
servant of Sarah's who obeyed Sarah's command to have sexual
intercourse with Abraham, so that they could have the son they
believed God had promised them. The problem was that what
Sarah did was completely against what God had spoken. Although
Hagar became pregnant by Abraham, Ishmael, the child that was
born as a result of their sexual union was not the son that God
had promised. As a result of their disobedience, Ishmael became
a source of trouble for Abraham, Sarah, and Isaac who was later
the son of promise. Because of their disobedience to God, Abraham and Sarah caused problems that could have been avoided,
and sadly, Hagar suffered because of their disobedience.

> "...So Abraham rose early in the morning and took bread and
> a bottle of water and gave them to Hagar, putting them on her
> shoulders, and he sent her and the youth away. And she wandered
> [aimlessly] and lost the way in the wilderness of Beersheba.
> When the water in the bottle was all gone, Hagar caused the youth
> to lie down under one of the shrubs. Then she went and sat down
> opposite him a good way off, about a bowshot, for she said, Let
> me not see the death of the lad. And as she sat down opposite
> him, he lifted up his voice and wept and she raised her voice and
> wept. And God heard the voice of the youth, and the angel of God
> called to Hagar out of heaven and said to her, What troubles you,

*Hagar? Fear not, for God has heard the voice of the youth where he is. Arise, raise up the youth and support him with your hand, for I intend to make him a great nation. Then God opened her eyes and she saw a well of water; and she went and filled the [empty] bottle with water and caused the youth to drink." **GENESIS 14–19***

In spite of their disobedience to Father, God blessed Ishmael and Hagar in the wilderness, but there is something key here that we must understand. God always gives His word before He does something significant. The sad thing is that Father has to search diligently for someone who is willing to listen to Him so that His plans may be carried out as He works with the person He chooses. Another sad thing is that in today's church we often fail to see the call of God on certain individuals and estrange them if they do not fit into our present church mold. We must understand that our heavenly Father doesn't just call men and women for the church of today but also for the church of tomorrow. Because He looks to the future, we often fail to understand that Father is working in the "now" preparing His church for the "not-yet". The way that we can understand this is to consider what is happening in prayer, seeking Father so that He may reveal to us what He is doing. There are many who are spared certain hardship because they listen to God, seek Him, and obey Him when He gives instructions.

"...The [reverent] fear of the Lord is clean, enduring forever; the ordinances of the Lord are true and righteous altogether. More to be desired are they than gold, even than much fine gold; they are sweeter also than honey and drippings from the honeycomb.

Moreover, by them is Your servant warned (reminded, illuminated, and instructed); and in keeping them there is great reward."
PSALM 19:9–11

Even though Ishmael was not the son that God promised to be Abraham's first born, he did come from Abraham's seed, so God promised to bless him. It was the act of disobedience that caused trouble in Abraham's home, when he and Sarah did not wait for Father's promise and moved ahead. Sarah was looking at her age and thinking that what God had said was impossible, but it was meant to be impossible. And whenever Father gives us instructions or speaks to us about those things that are impossible, His intention is to do the impossible through us. Seldom does our Father engage in conversation that does not require faith to hear. Because He is the Beginning and the Ending and the Author and Finisher of our faith, He speaks to the future often, causing our minds to project into the future, and increasing the faith in our hearts to accomplish what He has spoken. Dear ones, it is important to wait on God's timing, no matter what happens in times of struggle. Nothing happens to us that is not common for most every other person in this earth. Submission to God, especially during difficult times is absolutely necessary. This submission not only gives us the ability to resist the intrusion of Satan, but keeps our hearts alert and gives the Holy Spirit the ability to energize us.

"...For whatever is born of God is victorious over the world; and this is the victory that conquers the world, even our faith."
1 JOHN 5:4

If we are going to overcome what often overcomes us, then we will have to follow the prescription that our Father writes for us to overcome. We cannot simply hear Father speaking something or assume that He has spoken something and then try to make it happen in our own strength. We were created by God to work alongside Him. And as we work alongside Father, we begin to see that He created us to partner with Him, not as slaves, but as sons and daughters who are given instruction by Father and carry them out along with Him. This kind of intimate hearing, listening, obeying, and then seeing, produces the affirmation that we all need from God, and it keeps our spirits quiet and still. The more we spend time with Father in this type of intimate relationship, the quieter our spirits become. We can be still and silent within, whereas before we learned that our Father wants to have this kind of relationship with us, we were disquieted and searching within our souls for what our Father wants from us.

> "...For we are God's [own] handiwork (His workmanship), recreated in Christ Jesus, [born anew] that we may do those good works which God predestined (planned beforehand) for us [taking paths which He prepared ahead of time], that we should walk in them [living the good life which He prearranged and made ready for us to live]." **EPHESIANS 2:10**

It is wise to remember that God always knows where we are and that there is nowhere we can go where our Father and our God cannot find us. This knowledge that our Father knows everything should calm and quiet us, but the words that God speaks are not simply natural, they are also supernatural, producing the supernatural in our natural lives. Many of us walk in our natural strength, often opposing the strength, nature, and power of our Father in heaven, Who has given us the ability to live supernaturally.

Remember that during the times of struggle and difficulty that our Father is with us. He has allowed sustained difficulty in our lives that trains us to call upon Him, to look for Him, and to struggle to be with Him, so that we may find the strength that we need in adversity. This kind of seeking and finding will always produce within us the ability to be quiet and still as we wait to see what our Father is up to. And when we see the outcome, we begin to recognize and to better understand that our Father has been with us all along.

~~16

GETTING YOUR FOOTING

"He drew me up out of a horrible pit [a pit of tumult and of destruction], out of the miry clay (froth and slime), and set my feet upon a rock, steadying my steps and establishing my goings."
PSALM 40:2

Not everyone is called by God to public ministry, but whatever you are put in this world to do by God, then you should do it, regardless of whether that is public or not. The truth is that whatever you do for God, it is meant to somehow become public to some degree, meaning, that the good things we do for God seldom remain unknown. If we are truly doing the work that Christ has called us to do, then others will be influenced to do the same kind of work.

It should also be known that when our heavenly Father is dealing with us regarding ministry of any kind, His plans for us will oftentimes disagree with what we may have planned. In my own life I remember how, when the Lord first began dealing with me to move into the ministry that He was calling me to, I found it very difficult. The difficulty came from working with God Whom I could not see. I had to depend on Him to reveal Himself to me so that I could believe that it was His Spirit leading me. We can hear God's voice, but we must also learn how to share with others what God is speaking to us, and be able to share it with them in a way which they can understand. Oftentimes, some of the big mistakes that we make are those where we find ourselves trying to explain God. Knowing God is a process just as it is with any person or individual, so we must expect that it will take time to know God so that we may follow His instructions and better explain to others what He has spoken to us.

A lot is at stake when our heavenly Father begins to speak to us about ministry, especially if His plans are to dramatically change our living situation at the moment. There are so many questions to be answered: Where am I going? How will I do what you are telling me to do? Am I leaving all I've ever known behind? These are all very good questions and questions that Father can answer. Bear in mind that Father chooses us to be "sold out" to Himself, and in order for us to follow Him the way that He desires, we have to be willing to let go of our lives the way that we've known them so that we can gain our spiritual footing. When I speak of spiritual footing, I am talking about being able to know and understand from God where we are going and what He wants us to do. We cannot depend on people to know this for us, although we can learn more about this spiritual stability or footing when we are in the company of someone who has experience with God and consider them as a mentor.

If we are honest with ourselves, when someone remarks that God told them something, we often view this kind of comment with suspicion, when in reality, God does speak to us. He has to be able to speak to us so that He may lead us into what He has called us to do. He has to be able to make it clear to us where we are to go and keep our minds strong and healthy during the process by which we get to know Him and how He does things.

We also have to remember that when God speaks to us He is addressing us individually, thus the call of God upon our lives is an individual call. Knowing this before our heavenly Father begins to deal with us personally is very helpful; however we must be willing to surrender all of ourselves to Father, regardless of what He may tell us. It is wise to understand that when God calls us to any ministry, He already knows that this is what our lives were destined to become, so He is very much aware of how things should work out. But again, before we really know how this new calling works out in our lives, we have to learn how to be still and consider Him before we actually begin walking as mature Christians.

In the work that I do with the students in our Church Discipleship School, the Lord often makes me aware of the needs of the students, even before class starts. My focus must be on Father often so that I can recognize what He is showing me and realize that I cannot rely solely on myself to know what to do. When Father is telling our hearts to obey Him, we are often weak and afraid about what to do because we are not sure how Father works things out. Being still before God gives us the ability to know what He is planning and carrying out for our good. We have to quiet ourselves and not be afraid so that our heavenly

Father can share with us what we need to know and begin His ministry work in us. Truth be told, the Father begins His ministry work in us long before we actually begin the ministry itself. This kind of knowing and ministry planning by the Holy Spirit helps us to better know and to understand that Father has plans for us and that He is with us and will be with us in carrying out these plans of His.

When Father begins to call any of us into ministry, it will affect our lives dramatically. It could change most everything we know about ourselves, and even take us away from family members. But the more we respond to God the right way, we'll gain insight into how He wants us to do what we are called to, including being able to share with others what He is saying to us. The more we make sense to others as we learn how to carry out Father's will, the more we'll be able to explain to them what Father is speaking to us. While it may feel good to explain to others what Father is communicating to us, it might also be very helpful in carrying it out. So many well-meaning Christians have been derailed from Father's plans because someone in their lives did not understand what Father was calling them to do and caused them to question the validity of God's call. It is always wise to have good spiritual mentors in our lives, but it is also very important to understand that obeying God is very much between God and the person He is calling.

It may seem to be a very lonely journey to gain spiritual footing, but when we know that God is indeed calling us and we embrace this, then growing to know God more intimately becomes easier. But we cannot expect others, including those who may be very spiritual, to understand what we are going through as Father deals with us one-on-one. Be encouraged that God knows where we are at all times. His plans are designed to pull us into a stronger relationship with Him as well as others, so that during the times that I will refer to as the "tests" before the actual entering into the call, we will experience unrest. This kind of unrest is designed by God so that we may learn to find rest, stillness and quiet in Him. There will always be something going on around us that seems more urgent than what Father is calling us to do, but our primary goal in life should be to know God and to experience Him in every way we can, so that no matter what happens we can be still inwardly regardless of what is going on outwardly. The more we recognize God during the times when He is leading us a certain way, the more we will be able to have a spiritual and natural footing. They are both necessary in this life, but we do not have the ability to cause the spiritual and natural to agree just because we want to; only Father can do this.

17

APOLOGIZING TO GOD

"...Therefore [I now see] I have [rashly] uttered what I did not understand, things too wonderful for me, which I did not know...I had heard of You [only] by the hearing of the ear, but now my [spiritual] eye see You. Therefore I loathe [my words] and abhor myself and repent in dust and ashes." **JOB 42:3A, 5, 6**

"...I acknowledged my sin to You, and my iniquity I did not hide. I said, I will confess my transgressions to the Lord [continually unfolding the past till all is told]—then You [instantly] forgave me the guilt and iniquity of my sin. Selah [pause, and calmly think of that]!" **PSALM 32:5**

A confession is not always an apology. It can be an acknowledgement of a wrong doing, but it is how we act toward the person we confess to that genuinely says we are sorry. We do not apologize to someone and then continue to engage in the same behavior; otherwise, our apology really isn't sincere.

However, if we slip up and behave in a similar behavior unintentionally, then an apology can be acceptable. We all grow up progressively and not instantly. Yes, our heavenly Father is able to heal us of anything if He so chooses, but our heavenly Father enjoys the progress that we make when we lean on Him as we grow through difficulties. Matters of the heart can be so difficult to heal, but a humble spirit that is willing to accept responsibility for wrong doing in a broken relationship is always an excellent ingredient for reconciling harmed relationships. I have never seen any relationship in my life time that could not be reconciled. I have seen relationships where one or the other party refuses to forgive the other person involved because of the intensity of hurt that was done. In those cases, pride was the deciding factor, so the relationships were never reconciled. Suppose God treated us the way that we treat others? Forgiveness is a very powerful tool and Satan hates when we acknowledge our sinful acts toward others and repent. When we go further than simply acknowledging our wrong doing and ask for forgiveness in humility, God is given the ability through that humility to bring restoration. Although it may not happen immediately, a kind word turns away wrath. Apologies with humility brings about changed behavior in both parties. We must always remember that if we are going to make peace or be peace-makers, the kind that God talks about in Scripture, then we must understand that it doesn't matter who is right, but that what is right and that righteousness prevails. Righteousness in broken relationships is always what restores the two or more people to a healthy relationship. And this is possible if we surrender our hurt emotions to the Spirit of God.

How do we apologize to God? Many of us have felt that to apologize to God means to simply confess our sins to Him and allow Him to forgive us so that we can move past certain situations. While it is true that confession to God is necessary at times, we must remember that confession is for us, not for God. Father is already aware of what is in us and when or how we will fail. He already knows this and has provided a way through the blood of Jesus for our consciences to remain clear through confession. However, if we begin to view Father as a Person in our lives—a literal Person Who is God, then we will begin to sense and feel when His feelings are hurt. We know this instinctively because we are connected to His Spirit. God is not flesh and blood but spirit, and we are now, through Jesus Christ, part of that eternal spiritual connection with God. And if we are growing to know Father more intimately, then we recognize that He feels also. It is not only grief for our sins that our Father feels, but His emotions are like ours—in truth, He gave us our emotions. When we allow our emotions to yield to the Spirit of God, they function the way that Father intended, and we enjoy emotional health. When we are off-balance emotionally, it is usually because we've allowed ourselves to turn inward, trying to find the answer within our own hurt emotions, and we end up in the same cycle of not resolving those feelings that have been hurt. Apologizing and asking for forgiveness from God or from others is always a very healthy move. If our emotions are healthy then they are strong, and if our emotions are strong then they are quiet and at rest—they are still and ready to hear God speak quite easily and without much interference from emotions that are hurt and wounded. Forgiveness and confession allows the blood of Jesus to keep our souls clean so that we enjoy unin-terrupted communion with God. The more our souls are bare and clean before God, the easier it is to talk with Him and share our entire hearts and minds with Him. We then begin to see that Father is very interested in what we are going through and offers valid solutions to us when we are able to hear Him as our Father.

When is it that we become angry with God and pretty much dismiss His influence in our lives? In my years of experiencing God, the most common situation in which we have a falling-out with God is when He does not bless or honor the thing that we would like for Him to do. In our own hearts and minds we believe that what we would like to do is good and cannot find a reason for God not to honor what we believe is a good thing. We must remember that if God already has an established plan for our lives, then we cannot improve upon that plan, no matter how good we may think our plan may be. God never honors anything that does not honor Him, because He sees the potential danger in what we do and how it can cause sustained harm to us in the long term. Because God is able to see farther than we can, He will oftentimes set up roadblocks in our way so that we can-not accomplish certain things that we believe are good things. Because God does this we oftentimes blame Him for stopping us from enjoying life or wanting to do what we believe will give us joy or make our lives seem more worthwhile. Our heavenly Father is not into stopping us from enjoying life, but He is leading us into what He has planned for us that brings peace, rest, quiet-ness, and the ability to be still inside so that hearing and know-ing what He wants us to do becomes easier.

"...And in the course of time Cain brought to the Lord an offering of the fruit of the ground. And Abel brought of the firstborn of his flock and of the fat portions. And the Lord had respect and regard for Abel and for his offering, but for Cain and his offering He had no respect or regard. So Cain was exceedingly angry and indignant, and he looked sad and depressed. And the Lord said to Cain, Why are you angry? And why do you look sad and depressed and dejected? If you do well, will you not be accepted? And if you do not do well, sin crouches at your door; its desire is for you, but you must master it." **GENESIS 4:3–7**

God has a certain way that He wants things done. Oftentimes, we waste much of our lives trying to do things that please God and are let down in our feelings because, even with our best efforts, we still feel that God is not pleased with what we are doing.

Dear ones, it is not that God is displeased with us. We are told that without faith, it is impossible to please God. This literally means that without operating by faith, we cannot feel that God is pleased with us. We are justified through faith, and as we operate and function with God as His children, we experience the truest nature of what it means to operate by, through, and in faith. We learn from our experiences with God what pleases Him and what does not. The more we walk with God the clearer it becomes instinctively what we should do and what we shouldn't do. We learn that the closing of doors all around us does not come from God to keep us from enjoying life and having fun. Instead, He does this as a protective Father, Who is really trying to save us from wasting time in our lives so that we can move on to what He has designed us to do, which is really a lot of fun and enjoyable. But we cannot see His plans until we surrender our lives to Jesus Christ and stop choosing our own way.

Ministry. Many of us believe that when we find our ministry that we will be satisfied in life. We believe that some form of ministry work will cause us to be in favor with God, when in truth, God is far more concerned with our personal communion with Him. Intimacy and communion with God can sometimes be very difficult because our hearts remain guarded, often keeping the influence of the Holy Spirit at arms-length, because we are afraid of what God may require or ask us to do. But it is during the times of communion with God—being completely open and honest with Him, that we find out what Father wants us to do. He will tell us. He will show us and then work alongside us to accomplish it until we learn how to live in the new nature just as we have learned to live in the natural nature. Obeying God for all of His children should eventually become a naturally supernatural act, but it cannot as long as we try to instruct God and tell Him what we want to be in life. Not long ago the Lord gave me these words:

"...I do not want My people to live for the next open door or ministry opportunity, but to have intimacy with Me. When a man lives to know Me, He gains insight, rest, and learns that ministry is simply the by-product of knowing Who I am."

"The ministry that we do is an ongoing expression of our deepening love for Jesus, and is not intended to define us. As long as we look for God's affirming love in ministry or what we believe we are to do for God, we will continue to fall short in knowing who we really are from God's point of view. Ministry and work that God gives us is vitally important, but it should never be a substitute for the affirmation we get from being

alone with God that defines us as His children—something ministry cannot do."

The opening Scripture of this chapter is from Job. We remember all the difficulty that Job went through because of his faith in God. God knew the depth of Job's faith as He does with all of us. He also knows if the depth of our faith can stand up to the tests that Satan brings our way. The more we know God before we enter into any kind of test, the more power we know that we have access to. We also know that we are not alone because we have learned the power and presence of the Living God that we serve. Sometimes, however, as with Job and so many others who are growing to know God, we will make mistakes. We may think that God is harming us in some way, when in truth, God is leading us to a more intimate knowledge and awareness of Himself, which we can gain only through adversity and the tests that come into our lives that reveal what is really in our hearts. The more clearly we see what is in our hearts that opposes God and respond to it the way that Father wants us to respond to It, the less power Satan has over us. If Satan does not have power within us then he has much trouble tempting, testing, and drawing us away from God. God becomes clearer to us in what He does and does not do, when we have communion with Him. This is why we know that when we accuse God of being unfair or unrighteous, the tests that He prescribes for our lives show us the truth, and when we see this truth the way that Job did, we apologize. Nothing is wrong with being able to see our own sinful attitudes against God, but when we do see them against Father and others, we should always humble ourselves and make it right. The whole purpose of making this right is so that we may continue walking with God and enjoying Him. Our hearts are quieted and still before Him because of the work that we have allowed our Father to perform within us so that we may enjoy fellowship with Him and others.

> *"...Surely I have calmed and quieted my soul; like a weaned child with his mother, like a weaned child is my soul within me [ceased from fretting]."* **PSALM 131:2**

> *"...Return to your rest, O my soul, for the Lord has dealt bountifully with you."* **PSALM 116:7**

> *"...Let be and be still, and know (recognize and understand) that I am God."* **PSALM 46:10**